THE LOVE FACTOR

THE LOVE FACTOR

by
»Al Palmquist«
with Mandy Taylor

Thomas Nelson Publishers
Nashville

Contents

This story is fictionalized, based on the true accounts of four young girls who were involved in prostitution. Some names have been changed, some incidents altered to insure the anonymity of certain individuals.

»1«

The Kid Who Became a Hooker

"Yes, ma'am. Yes. I understand how difficult.... Not for twenty-four hours, right. If you haven't heard anything by four o'clock tomorrow afternoon, call us again. Yes. We'll be on the lookout for her, but officially there's nothing.... That's all right. Yes, I have your number. Try not to worry now. Good night."

I hung up and the phone lines carried the distraught parent away, back to deal with her agony alone. My scrawled notes reflected an old version of an even older story: Rebecca Ann Lowry, five foot three inches, age fifteen, last seen leaving Park High at 3:10 P.M., wearing blue jeans, a blue plaid shirt, tennis shoes, with maybe five bucks on her. Her family had quarreled the night before, friends claimed to know nothing of her whereabouts, and she hadn't shown up at an aunt and uncle's place in the north suburbs. Now her parents were beginning to panic so they called me.

Officially, I had said, nothing could be done until Rebecca had been gone one day. Nevertheless, I tossed the note onto a pile of mail and messages I would get to later. I have a special interest in teenaged runaways. I'm a cop.

I leaned back in the creaking old wood and leather desk chair, the kind used in late night detective movies, and slowly rolled my head from one shoulder to the other, pressing against the tired muscles. My eyes passed over the vacant desks surrounding me in the office—all piled high, like mine, with papers and other clutter—over the clock— almost 2:00 A.M.—then skimmed the letters of the Juvenile Division sign on the frosted glass of the door, backward to me but clear enough to anyone outside, then came to rest on a window across the room.

It was an unusually black June night out there. Black and dead. That's what the window said, but I didn't believe it. I stretched again, then surrendered to the lure of the glass-restrained night and walked over. The street below me repeated the lie; all was quiet and still. All of Minneapolis seemed quiet and still tonight. I remembered how a friend had described police work once: total boredom sprinkled with moments of sheer panic. When the rest of us complained that movies and TV shows were too unrealistic, he always said, "Oh, they're realistic, all right. They just pack six months' action into a half hour!"

I turned around to lean on the window frame and yawned, wishing I could drive home right now and snuggle into bed next to Gayle, my wife of eight years. I supposed I would have to wrestle Jenny off my side first, but she would settle for a little friendly scratching behind the ears and a spot on the rug beside me. A huge collie, Jenny had no aspirations toward becoming a guard dog; she loved people too much.

Out in the hall, I heard a faint disturbance growing into a commotion and then a small war erupted through the door. The war was mostly skin-colored with plainclothesmen flanking either side. It wrenched, cursed, kicked, bit, and screamed, creating a threat to anyone in range.

"Settle down, little lady!" ordered one of the undercover men. "Just take it easy." Officer Scotty Thompson may as well have talked to a whirlwind.

It was a lady-war, then. I noted that the two husky officers had employed a pair of handcuffs.

"Cuffs, huh?" I observed, walking over to help. "You must have, oh, at least ninety-five pounds hooked here!"

The men glanced at me and without a word, as though they had rehearsed it, released the girl's arms simultaneously. The quick action caught her off guard, and she began to fall. Instinctively my hands shot out to catch her, but I missed. Taking lightning advantage, she hit the floor and made a direct lunge for my ankles. The tactic succeeded; I received a hearty bite in the shins.

"Ow!" I shrieked, grabbing the assaulted limb, a maneuver which forced me to hop. "You're a real sweetheart, aren'tcha, kid?" Since I am tall—six foot three—I must have looked like an unbalanced whooping crane. Although the pain was incredible, the humiliation was worse.

"She's all yours, Al," Officer Ray Warden said dryly, a twinkle playing over his features. "Shouldn't give you much trouble. Most of the fight's gone out of her by now."

Scotty belly-laughed. I struggled to maintain my balance on one leg while trying to stay clear of The Biter, who was still knee-walking somewhere below me.

"I am really happy," I retorted miserably, "you guys can find some small pleasure in your dull and tedious work." I finally limped out of reach and the girl scrambled to her feet. "Where'd you find her, anyway?"

They had picked her up on Fifth and Hennepin after she had mistakenly propositioned Ray who had acted as a customer, or "john," soliciting sexual services for pay. "We read her her rights..." said Scotty.

"Loud and clear," interjected Ray, referring to the ruckus she must have created on the street.

"... and that's all we know. She wouldn't talk."

The two young officers combed their hair, straightened and tucked in their shirts, pulled up their socks and nursed their own bruises for a few minutes. Then Ray began to walk toward the girl. She stiffened, her eyes narrowing.

11

"I just want my cuffs back," he said, none too kindly. "Now turn around and stand still."

She did what everyone does when relieved of the heavy shackles: she rubbed her wrists. When she turned to face us again, I was close enough to grab her in case she decided to make a break for it. She was my prisoner now and knew it. Defiantly she stepped back, away from me. There she stood her ground and glared.

"Well," Scotty said wearily, "let's get some coffee and tackle the arrest report, huh?"

"Sounds good," Ray answered, eyes on me. He was asking nonverbally if I could handle the girl alone.

I nodded. "Anyway, Pete's next door," I assured Ray with a lowered voice. I was not worried about trouble from her, but I might need help with the phone if we got busy. "Just have him check in later."

"Right."

Predictably, the phone jangled as soon as the door closed behind them. Telephones, I believe, have personalities of their own, usually perverse. They know when people enter the bathroom, sit down to a meal, or have guests over.

I ventured a few more steps on the wounded leg, answered the phone, and kept watch on my prisoner. She stood, hands planted on her hips. My brief business concluded, I replaced the receiver and gave her my full attention. She was probably sixteen years old with long, natural blond hair. Her breathing, accelerated from our skirmish, had returned to normal and she appeared subdued. Her feet were stationed firmly and she leveled at me the hardest set of eyes I had ever faced. I tried to remember that she was a kid and cops are not supposed to be intimidated by kids.

She was obviously a hooker. Tight white shorts, rolled high on her thighs, spidery little spiked heels, sheer black blouse, and layers of makeup. But something about her didn't add up. I studied her eyes again—"mirror of the soul," someone has said. They were cold and flinty, but they were giving away her secret; for under the heavy, iridescent eyelids I was suddenly startled to discover a child standing in front of me. A little girl was hiding under all the lipstick and false lashes and mascara. How could any man be sexually attracted to this kid, this baby? The thought repulsed me. She looked like a fugitive from her mother's dressing table. This was no sixteen-year-old.

With professional detachment—words I'd heard from my Police Academy instructor—I picked up my heart and put it back where it belonged. I had two children at home who needed all the fathering I could give them. Here, I was a cop with a job to do.

I cleared my throat. It was a signal, one I hoped would be heavy with implication: You are in trouble, you are in the hands of the law, we've had enough of your tantrums, now straighten up and cooperate. With that one very significant sound, I advanced deliberately toward the prisoner.

I limped deliberately, actually. And when I reached my creaky chair, I gratefully seized the back for support. The mood I had hoped to create was suffering but I cleared my throat once more and looked sternly at the kid.

She was nowhere near laughing, but a flicker of amusement did seem to be tickling the corners of her ridiculously red mouth.

"What's your name?" I began in a no-nonsense tone.

The defiant, silent stare was her only response.

Slowly and carefully, I brought over a chair which I slid alongside her legs, then resumed my position with one hand resting on my chairback. We continued to stand.

The silence made me self-conscious but I did not move. She did not move. Two pairs of eyes locked in fierce combat for power. The clock murmured with electricity. This silent tactic usually worked for me, as I was a veteran victor of the old "Blink-Stare-You-Down" game from my youth, but apparently I was up against a real pro here.

Just when I thought I would have to try something else, she melted into the chair and spat out, "Kimberly." It was the first word she hadn't screamed.

"What's your last name?" I asked evenly, intent on preserving my fragile victory.

Her icy eyes regarded me again while she nibbled at the inside of her left cheek. Then Kimberly leaned forward and said very clearly, "Pringle. Kimberly Pringle, Officer."

"Officer" was an obscenity to her. Miss Kimberly Pringle sat back smugly and waited for my reaction to this news.

I reached for a pen as my mind fumbled with the name. Pringle. Pringle. Then I knew.

"Pringle, huh? You Inspector Pringle's kid?"

She was. "The old . . . he's my father." "Father" was an obscenity, too.

"How old are you?" I asked. If I thought she was responding to me out of intimidation, I was wrong. This kid was playing a game. We would play by her rules. And if I wasn't mistaken, her father would be the trophy. Well, I could play as long as she could. She was deliberating over her age, so I warned, "I can look it up, you know."

She decided to play it straight. "Thirteen."

This was 1971, at the beginning of a terrible, sick trend to use younger and younger children for sexual service. Nothing could be worse. We would grow to call it "kiddy porn," and one day a thirteen-year-old prostitute would be considered quite typical. But with this child standing before me, I could not even fathom what I was hearing.

"Thirteen?" I repeated incredulously. "Thirteen? You have two older sisters who . . . ?"

Her lips curled in disgust.

So Dewey Pringle—Inspector Dewey Pringle—had provided the world a third prostitute from his own family. Why? Why did three daughters become three prostitutes—and from a cop's family, too? How could the Inspector let it happen? Inspector Pringle was neither a friend nor a model cop. Apparently he was not a father, either. I reached for the phone.

Dewey must have been sleeping hard because I waited six rings for his muffled, "Ynngh," at the other end.

"Inspector Dewey Pringle?"

"Ynngh . . ."

"This is Officer Palmquist in Juvenile. Sorry to disturb you. You awake?"

"Mmmgh."

"Inspector, we've just arrested your daughter . . . ah, Kimberly . . . for prostitution. We have her here in Juvenile now."

Only silence greeted the news. Finally I said, "Inspector?" A distant oath came back before the receiver was slammed down.

I winced with the fresh pain in my right ear. The Pringles were clearly bent on my destruction tonight. Quietly I replaced the receiver and waited for the ache to subside. I tried to feel sorry for Dewey Pringle, but the sympathy wouldn't come. I knew too much about him.

With a deep breath I turned to face Kimberly again and found fire blazing in her eyes. There was not a trace of fear or shame, only white-hot hatred.

"How did you get into prostitution?" I began again, pen in hand.

"I ain't talkin' no more," she said, clamping her lips together.

Sure you will, Kimberly, I vowed silently. Aloud I said, "Well, then, I'll have to lock you up for the night." I looked across the room toward a temporary holding cell which several handyman-type cops had constructed from an unused office. It looked like any other office, but it had a strong lock and a small, eye-level window had been added to the door; inside was one chair. I stood up to escort my prisoner to the cell.

"Will you feed me?" Kimberly asked quickly.

"No." I was at her elbow and gripped her arm firmly, lifting her. Naturally, prisoners were fed regularly, but Kimberly apparently didn't know that, and I would be off duty before her breakfast would arrive. It was a technicality, and I moved out of her view so she couldn't see a tiny grin. When I had her on her feet, she braced her tottering little shoes against my strength.

"All right, all right, you bully pig cop!" she raged, skidding a little on the smooth tile. "What do you want to know, anyway? I don't know nothin'!"

"What were you doing on Fifth and Hennepin at 1:30 in the morning? Curfew is at 10:00 P.M." I allowed her to sit down again, then faced her.

Kimberly looked at me in contempt. "I'm a big girl, sir," she mocked.

"Big enough to be hooking for a living?"

She had nothing to say and dropped her eyes. She had been caught in the act of propositioning and didn't try to deny it. But was there a trace of shame here? I couldn't figure her. She hated her father, she hated cops, yet she was quite willing to talk. The tough front she presented was merely a ploy. She was using me, but for what?

"Is this your first offense, Kimberly?"

"Yes."

"Do you live at home?"

"Yah. Mostly. Sometimes I stay with a . . . friend."

"Girl friend or boy friend?"

Kimberly raised her head now and looked at me. She hesitated. "Girl friend," she lied.

I returned a skeptical gaze. "It's true!" she asserted loudly.

"A girl friend. Her name is . . . Sandie. It's Sandie, really. Sandie Johnson."

"Where does Sandie live?" I asked.

"Oh, on Fortieth or something. I never asked her. I don't know for sure."

I pressed harder. "What's her father's name?"

"Can't remember. I think she lives alone. Yah, alone."

She was as poor a liar as I had ever interrogated. She answered a few questions about school, her friends, her usual activities, how long she'd been prostituting—a little over three months—even questions about some of her customers.

Several times she looked at the clock, but I didn't ask why. I figured we both knew.

Once, when I asked if she had a pimp, Kimberly stiffened and sent me a chilly warning with those expressive eyes. *Off limits,* the look said clearly. We wouldn't talk about pimps, period. "No," she lied fiercely.

Something in the air tensed a little more each time Kimberly checked the clock. I felt it and found myself growing silent, expectant, watching the clock, too. When a shiver made her tremble, I walked over, with only a slight limp, and reached for an old pink sweater that had one day taken up residence on one of our coat hooks. Kim made a face at our Official Pink Sweater but she arranged it snugly over her shoulders. I answered the phone a couple of times and shuffled papers on the desk. And waited.

Suddenly Kimberly leaped to her feet and began to back slowly across the room, eyes intent on the clouded glass of the door. She'd heard it before I had, the sound of familiar footsteps.

His shadow preceding him, Inspector and father Dewey E. Pringle arrived.

17

»2«

Quirks, Naps, and Drinking Habits

I had heard stories about Dewey Pringle since my first day on the force. He was loud, a big talker, especially regarding all the ladies he took to bed. He solved an amazing number of crimes. And turned in truly unbelievable police work. He said. Often.

But some of the cops told their own tales about Dewey. One was about the night Dewey and ten or twelve cronies decided to take over the police department. The way I heard it, they'd all gotten together at Happy Jack's after their shift. They had several rounds of drinks so they were feeling pretty good when the inspiring idea came to Dewey.

"You know," he had said, "I used to be the Dep'ty Chief in thish . . . city," and his arm swept broadly to indicate the Minneapolis geography. The unfortunate guy next to Dewey, however, was just lifting a beer to his lips. Dewey's arm collided squarely with the full mug, dousing the man and throwing them both off balance.

"'Scuze me," Dewey mumbled, and tried to mop his friend with a napkin—an action which only threatened anew to upend them both.

Further down the bar, Dewey's close friend, Harvey, who had missed the action, lifted high his own draught while coughing gustily. "I think," he announced with ceremony, "that Dewey is our man for the next Deputy Chief. Let's hear it, men!"

There was much cheering and backslapping then, but Dewey seemed, somehow, to have disappeared. The story goes that a neighboring party of rabble rousers saw Dewey crawling about on the floor, having been decked by an enthusiastic but poorly aimed handshake, and thought a fight had broken out. Not to be left out of the fun, they rose to the occasion and in ten minutes the bar was in shambles.

The excitement proved too much for Dewey—at this point my storytellers always lowered their voices to preserve a shred of dignity—and he thoroughly dampened himself in his frantic search for the door. Battered, bruised, and barely conscious, Dewey's campaign partners were last seen holding down the floor. Undoubtedly, the story had taken on some embellishment; still, no one ever again heard Dewey talk about taking over the police department.

The story about Dewey's most celebrated stakeout I heard from a South Side officer. Patroling Lake Street in his squad car one evening, he spotted what looked like a stalled vehicle. It was parked at an odd angle, its backside blocking an entire lane of traffic. Investigating, the officer observed a large man slumped over the wheel.

It was Dewey. Drunk Dewey. Bored Dewey, who had sipped a bit too much while on an uneventful stakeout. He had passed out in an unmarked police car.

Angry and embarrassed professionally, the officer quickly escorted Dewey back to his own division downtown with a warning that next time he'd be thrown in jail with the rest of the drunks.

Lots of cops drink and I suppose some pass out now and then. But Dewey was the only one I'd known to succumb while on duty in his vehicle.

When it came to an honest day's work, no other police

supervisor could do as little, yet look as exhausted, as Dewey. He would sit forlornly behind a desk piled high with unfinished business, wearing his martyr look. Apparently he felt he really owed himself a nap, so every afternoon at about 1400 hours—two o'clock—he dozed off.

One day, Lieutenant Dan Forbes, a friend and a fine cop, came to my desk to ask about something I'd written on a report. My handwriting tends to be of a liberated variety. Dan was not acquainted with Dewey's afternoon habit, so, coming upon the slumbering supervisor, he thought Dewey could be suffering a heart attack. Dan sprang into action, jerking back Dewey's head and assuming the posture for mouth-to-mouth resuscitation.

Instantly Dewey was awake, staring point-blank into two enormous eyes.

"What's the big..." Dewey started, then recognized the lieutenant's uniform. Startled, Dan vaulted backward, tripping over a chair.

"I was, ah, we, ah, had a long. . . ." Dewey's voice trailed off and I watched his neck and ears redden. Cops in the room smirked. Dan narrowed his eyes, pursed his lips, squared his shoulders, and looked down at Dewey for a long, long time. Finally he turned and left.

The trauma did not keep Dewey from taking his daily snooze, but he never enjoyed it fully after that. He was pretty jumpy, and the area near his desk was the scene of any number of noisy "accidents." A large bolt dropped into a metal wastebasket near the sleeping form became the favorite.

Dewey developed a practice of writing general orders that could not possibly be understood. The men, however, didn't worry much about it; those caught ignoring an order simply acted perplexed and said, "Huh, I didn't know that's what you meant!" If Dewey tried to explain it, he usually tangled it up even more, and then took to muttering as he walked away. It became a challenge to the guys to see who could get Dewey the most confused.

Dewey's little quirks or naps or even his drinking habits weren't what made him so hard to take, however. It was his attitude. He swaggered through life, bragging about the women he'd had, how many tough cases he had solved, how many times he had been a hero. A subject he never mentioned, however, was his family. His wife, it was said, had run off with a used car dealer, and now all three daughters were gainfully employed as hookers.

»3«

"How Could She Do It?"

All these images of Inspector Dewey E. Pringle sprinted through my head in about thirteen seconds while Kimberly and I, like frozen statues, stood with our eyes fixed on the door. Staccato footsteps had grown louder and louder before halting outside. Next we saw a burly shadow through the glass.

With a crashing burst, then, the waiting was over. Dewey looked like a nightmare. If I could have ignored his angry face, I might have howled in laughter. An old pair of black patent leather dress shoes, sporting the heel taps which accounted for the loud clicking, had been pulled onto bare feet. A hairy stretch of ankle led to the hem of baggy jogging pants. The lengthwise stripe which had torn loose from one pantleg flapped wildly as he walked. A festive, flowered Hawaiian shirt bloomed on the upper portion of his body; tangled, matted hair provided a nestlike look on Dewey's head.

But at that point, I was forced to look at his face and any impulse to laugh vanished. Sleep had distorted Dewey's face into a wrinkled, red, puffy mass, and his fury contorted the muscles into something that belonged in a horror show. I cringed and glanced at Kimberly. She seemed to have turned to stone.

Dewey snorted as he stood glaring at her. I had never felt

so helpless in my life. Legally, I had no right to keep them apart. She was a juvenile and he was the parent. Furthermore, he was my superior. For me to interfere would be insubordination. Besides, he would not dare to beat her up, not in the precinct office. Maybe it was all an act. Yet, my heart pumped harder and my stomach tightened in apprehension. I had never seen Dewey like this.

Dewey's show of anger was having its desired effect. Two other officers, sensing trouble, had followed Dewey into Juvenile; we now looked silently from Dewey to each other and back to Dewey. The moment grew longer, the air more tense, and I prayed the phone would ring or something. Dewey had crossed the threshold but advanced no further. He just glared and softly wheezed.

When about two years had gone by like this—it may have been closer to forty-five seconds—the two other policemen and I couldn't take any more. I doubt that any of us wanted to grow old staring at Dewey and Kimberly Pringle. One of them coughed and shuffled his feet on the tile; the other picked up a newspaper and shook it out. By the time I had steered my chair, which creaked and complained very nicely for me, back to where it belonged, Dewey's show was over.

He pawed at the floor one last time as I sat down, then he lunged at her. I came straight out of my chair again when he reached Kimberly. He clamped one burly hand around her arm and manhandled her into the holding cell.

I caught a glimpse of her face before she disappeared. What I expected—pain, fear, anger, perhaps more indignant cursing—was not there. She had instead a sense of resignation. This was obviously not the first time she had experienced her father's wrath.

Dewey slammed the door behind them, as though emphasizing his private rights as her parent.

I was helpless. Absolutely helpless. I breathed a lot and prayed, "Oh, Kimberly," and sat down in utter misery and stood up again and sat down again. I turned my back on the cell and covered my face.

There were no screams. There were slaps and bumps and Dewey's cursing, but no feminine screams. There was the shuddering of the wall, a man's shouting accusations, and the crashing of the chair onto the floor, but no feminine screams.

I could hardly breathe. I was suffocating in wrath. When I heard one long agonizing cry, I flew out of my chair. Dewey had to be stopped, rights or no rights.

In those days, some divisions had not yet traded their manual typewriters for electric ones. Juvenile's faithful, ancient model usually sat back against the wall out of the way. But on this rueful night the machine was perched on the edge of my desk, its long return arm extending into the room.

As I leaped up, the return arm became hooked on my belt buckle. The typewriter bravely hung on, throwing me off balance. My mind was on the holding cell so I was barely conscious of my frantic jerking one way and another to rid myself of the heavy machine.

Finally I had to unscramble my thoughts, bend my knees, slam the typewriter firmly down on the desktop and hold it there as I squatted further to maneuver my buckle free of the monster.

In all, I had wasted only a few seconds, but I was sure Kimberly was dead. I tore across the floor, reached for the doorknob, and was nearly knocked down by a mighty outward thrust.

Dewey, flushed and sweating, erupted from the cell in a fury. Unseeing, he swept past me with the bitter commentary, "How could she do this to me? I've been a good father to her. Done all a man can do. How could she do it to me?" No sound came from the holding cell.

I stared at his retreating back, unable to funnel both thoughts into my one mind: This huge man had just roughed up his thirteen-year-old child, yet *he* was the injured party! As a final exclamation, Dewey's fist smashed hard into the door frame. Then he stood fuming, cursing at the floor, before going back out into the night.

I hurled heated insults at Dewey through the door. I spat at him. Adrenaline coursed through my veins and without restraint I spent all my venom on him. I told him what kind of father he was and warned him not to cross my path again. And I shook with fury.

I delivered my entire discourse just below hearing level, however. The two cops apparently were watching the veins on my neck pulsating. One said kindly, "How about some coffee, Al?"

Slowly my head cleared and I became aware of them. They were angry, too. I closed my eyes, inhaled a long deep breath and nodded slightly. "Thanks. See if you can find Pete, would you?" I added.

An awful fear nagged at me and I tried to place it. It had something to do with Dewey's departure. The picture began to take shape: that closed fist against the framework. If that fist had been used on Kimberly. . . .

There was still no sound from the cell directly behind me. I whirled to the door and flung it wide open. The pink sweater lay off to one side. I bent down to pick up a thin, tapered stick—it was a broken heel. A noiseless form curled on the floor in the far corner, knees drawn up, arms covering the head, and stringy blond hair sprawled all around the scrawny arms and shoulders. I saw no movement.

I knelt over her and gently began to pry the child's arms away from her face. Her resistance reassured me. She wasn't unconscious, at least.

"Kimberly," I said, "Where does it hurt? Should I get a doctor?" I was still shaking with anger.

Kimberly groaned faintly and began to uncurl. I eased the hair away from her face and inspected the nose, the jaw, the forehead. Her lip was getting puffy, and she allowed me to touch one spot near her eye that was bleeding a little. She winced but it appeared to be only a scrape. My white handkerchief—a recent gift from my wife, with the initials "AP" monogrammed in the corner—blotted up the tiny beads of blood.

"How about the rest of you?" I asked. "Does anything feel broken?"

She tested her joints slowly and touched several painful spots, moaning as she did. These areas I checked quickly too, but felt sure she would not need immediate medical attention. Finally I sat down on the floor and began to unwind.

"Do you want to see a doctor, Kim?" I asked once more.

She moved her head just enough to signal no.

I heard Pete come in. "Al?" he called.

"Here."

There were hurried footsteps, then he filled the doorway. "She O.K.?" he asked after a moment.

"No," I sighed, "she's not. She's not O.K. at all. She's hurting inside and out, I imagine."

Kimberly looked up sharply as I spoke, then turned to acknowledge Pete.

"Hi," he said, smiling. She did not move. "Do you need a doctor?"

"Uh uh," she replied with finality, obviously weary of answering that question, and laid her head down again.

Pete looked at me. "You all right?"

"Sure."

"Can you handle her?"

I nodded.

"Your coffee is on the desk. I'll watch the phone."

"Thanks."

Pete left, and I tried to figure out what to do. Dewey had left no instructions, and Kimberly did not really need to be admitted to the hospital. Yet this bare cell was hardly adequate for a child who had been beaten. I looked at her. What she needed was Gayle. Gayle would clean her up, feed her, give her a motherly hug, and put her to bed.

Kimberly shifted positions on the hard floor. "Do you hate my father?" she asked bluntly.

"Why do you want to know?" I asked after awhile.

"I just don't think you like him much," she replied. She was silent again. Then, softly, "Does your ankle still hurt?"

"Nah. You're too puny to do much damage," I said. A rush of tenderness enveloped me and I wondered what my academy instructors would do with their professional detachment if they had been here.

"Kimberly, if you like, I can find you something to drink and let you get some sleep. We have a cot down the hall in. . . ."

"No."

I looked at her.

"I want a drink of water but I'm not movin' any more." She moaned as she turned slowly onto her stomach. Had she not been in pain, I would have gathered her into my arms. I wanted to comfort her and protect her and guide her little life along a kinder, more gentle path. My eyes suddenly welled up with tears and it was an effort to swallow. She needed a real daddy.

"O.K.," I said, getting to my feet. "But you can have the cot whenever you want it." Spotting the sweater, I picked it up, shook off a fluff of dust, and covered as much of Kimberly as I could. Then I went to look for water and a blanket.

I saw my coffee steaming on my desk. "Thanks," I said to Pete, who was still in the office, talking with two uniformed officers. Officer Jay Johnstone seemed to be enjoying a private joke. I looked at him curiously and he grinned wider.

It took only a minute to round everything up. I ducked back into the cell-turned-infirmary to administer the water, slip a pillow under Kimberly's head, and tuck a blanket around her. Her eyes were sad and vacant. She did try to smile but the effort broke open her lip again, and she pressed my handkerchief to the cut. Then she shut her eyes. I did not see how she could be comfortable, but decided it would be O.K. for a couple of hours' sleep. Kids sleep on the floor sometimes just for fun, I reasoned lamely.

There was another little drama developing as I left Kimberly. Jay Johnstone was on the phone and glanced up when he saw me; he still had that grin on his face. Officer Dave Thompson looked forlorn, as though he had been left out of the fun.

"Who *is* that?" Thompson demanded.

"Hey, Pumtwist," Pete interrupted. He had invented the nickname and seldom called me anything else. His use of "Al" earlier had been a sign of concern. "How's the kid?"

"She'll make it," I replied. "I told her to get some sleep. She needs it."

"Don't we all," Pete cracked. "O.K. if I go wrap up, then?" Pete was gathering statistics for a runaway report and I knew he wanted to finish tonight.

I waved him away. Pete Blake and I had been partners for eight weeks. We made a good team and Pete could usually find something to laugh about in every situation. Good cops need a healthy balance, and I respected Pete's cool head and his good heart.

Thompson opened his mouth in my direction again. I needed that coffee. Walking to my desk I rolled my head back and forth across my shoulders, the best remedy I'd found for working out tension and weariness. The coffee was still pretty hot and, strangely, tasted great even though I am not a coffee drinker.

Thompson had spoken. "That was Inspector Pringle, right?" he'd asked, and now he thumped a pencil onto his palm impatiently.

I nodded.

"And there is a girl in the cell, right?"

"Right."

That was the extent of Thompson's knowledge and he sat mutely, waiting for me to take it from there. I began to answer just as I heard Johnstone say into the phone, "I'll tell him, Mrs. Lowry. Don't worry, we will. I hope you folks can work it out, now. All right, good night."

The "Lowry" part interested me, and I looked at Johnstone.

"Know something about a Lowry kid?" he asked. "Rebecca Ann Lowry?"

I nodded.

"She made it home. Tanked up but glad to be back. Some guy scared her pretty bad. Probably a pimp, from the sound of it. I didn't ask too many questions. The mother was already crying."

Well, things were looking up. A runaway safely back home was one less prostitute. Or dead body.

Thompson was about to explode. He was a young, ex-Marine drill sergeant with only six months' police experience, and he felt insecure if he didn't know everything about everybody. Jay Johnstone, his partner, was a seasoned, twenty-three-year veteran with plenty of street moxie. If Thompson settled down and developed a little patience, the older man could teach him to be the best cop in the business. Almost everyone respected Jay Johnstone. Almost everyone.

Johnstone leaned toward me. "Palmquist," he said, "I just want to know one thing. Is that his kid?" He jabbed a thumb in the direction of the cell.

"Yah. Kimberly." I sipped my coffee.

"Whose kid?" Thompson demanded again. "Who is that in there? Whose kid?" He sounded like a broken record.

A look crept over Johnstone's face exactly like the look my son had when I announced that he would get a bike for Christmas. Thompson watched, his mouth gaping. I'd have put him out of his misery but Johnstone wanted this moment for himself. Turning to Dave, he reported, "We just busted Pringle's kid for hooking!" Holding his breath he looked at me for confirmation.

I nodded soberly.

It was a triumphant instant and Johnstone began to laugh, louder and louder until I looked with alarm toward the cell. Johnstone understood the hint but his emotions refused to be quieted. Covering his mouth to muffle the racket, Johnstone bounded up and down, pounding his leg and carrying on like the people on TV game shows.

Poor Thompson. He couldn't have been more shocked if he'd gotten a pie in the face. Eyes glued on the senior officer, he moved, trancelike, toward me, giving Johnstone a wide berth. "What's he doing?" he whispered hoarsely. "He's cracked up, hasn't he? Is this how it happens?"

I laughed then. Most of us had seen Jay Johnstone in one of his rare humors, but this was Thompson's first demonstration.

"What?" Thompson asked when I began to laugh, too. "What's the matter? How come you're laughing?" Nervously he looked again at Jay, who was still capering around. "Al, come on now. Don't laugh. Please." He sounded near panic.

"Oh, he's all right," I assured Dave. "I think he's just found something he's been looking for for a long time."

"What? What's he been looking for? Are you sure? Al, he's never been like this before. What do you mean, anyway? All we found here is a teenage hooker. He hasn't been looking for a teenage hooker! Does it have something to do with the Inspector?" Thompson leaned against the desk, exhausted. "I don't know. I think he's crazy, I really do. He's gone buggy."

"Dave," I said, "you're too high-strung to be a cop. Believe me, Jay Johnstone is as sane as you are. Maybe more." I grinned and patted his shoulder.

Eventually Johnstone got it all out of his system. He

gulped the rest of his coffee, then said he had to see a guy about a dog. I chuckled. It was a phrase I hadn't heard in years and it meant, in this case, his news was too good to keep, that he was off to spread the word about Dewey. He told Thompson to stay with me for a few minutes, he'd be right back. At the door he cautioned, "Don't let Palmquist convert you, kid." Then he was gone.

Thompson frowned at me. "That's right," he said, "you're a preacher, aren't you?"

I nodded and grinned. "A preacher-cop. How's that for a combination? But it's not a disease, Thompson!" Then I told him briefly about the church I'd served for several years before going to work for Teen Challenge in New York. "I like preaching and I like 'copping,'" I concluded. "I want to do 'em both!"

Thompson was eager to learn about Pringle, however, so I made myself comfortable and told him what I knew.

» 4 «

Not Much of a Cop

Jay Johnstone and Dewey Pringle had come on the job at the same time about twenty-three years ago. They'd walked a beat together when most cops still had beats; there were only a few squad cars around then.

Johnstone was a quiet man, but smart and alert. Everyone he worked with came to respect him deeply. Almost everyone. Dewey, by comparison, was a showy bigmouth who earned respect from no one.

(Officer Thompson eagerly nodded his head in anticipation.)

The detectives used to say of Dewey that he couldn't find a wounded elephant in a fresh snowfall. But whenever a good piece of police work was turned in by the Johnstone-Pringle team, Dewey managed to take credit for it.

Dewey used to brag for hours—the years had not changed him—about how he busted all the holdup men, how he stopped all the burglars, and how he solved all the crimes.

He'd had a group of ladies around him in a Lake Street bar one night where he'd done more than his usual amount of elbow bending, telling them how he had brilliantly apprehended a supermarket robber by wrestling him to the ground and seizing his sawed-off shotgun.

The truth was, however, Officer Johnstone had made the bust while Dewey hid outside the store until it was over.

"You mean Johnstone was alone in the store with the holdup man?" asked Thompson. "Dewey didn't even back him up?"

Yah, yah, Thompson had the picture.

"Well, why didn't Johnstone blow the whistle on him? Why didn't he shut him up?"

No, Johnstone isn't that way. He'd never do that. He'd do his job and keep his mouth shut.

Well, it wasn't too many years before Dewey had landed a sit-down day job by helping a friend into office. (Dewey's help was underhanded but effective. Going from bar to bar on his beat, Dewey would run his mouth about the "honest new councilman this city needed," and the drunks bought it. The honest new councilman was a crook but he ended up in the councilman's seat, nevertheless. And Dewey sat down to a soft desk job.)

Dewey's new job was in Licensing. He processed the city licenses, including liquor licenses. Everybody soon noticed that Dewey was becoming the best dressed cop in town. He'd even switched from three-two beer to the finest Scotch. Eyebrows were raised over his expensive new tastes although nothing illegal was ever proven. But anyone could figure out Dewey was receiving money under the table.

With his new clothes and cash came a new circle of women. The joke was that Dewey no longer had to settle for the coarse, vulgar drunks in the corner bars. Now he hung around with the richer, bored drunks in finer lounges. And still he bragged. For hours Dewey went on about all the ladies he'd taken to bed. Those stories were an obsession with him.

"Until tonight, I guess Dewey Pringle thought he had everyone fooled," I said, leaning back. "You see, when his wife ran off, Dewey just said she was no good. Put all the blame on her. And his two other girls went away to college before they began hooking. So Dewey could blame the college or their friends or their left-wing political beliefs." I sighed. "But who's he going to blame for his thirteen-year-old kid getting into prostitution right under his nose? How long can he keep blaming everyone and everything else?"

Thompson leaned back, studying me without really seeing me, in his effort to comprehend everything. "So when you said Johnstone finally found something he'd been looking for. . . ."

I finished for him. "Johnstone finally got something on Pringle. Something big enough to make up for some of the dirt of the past."

"What will he do about it?" Thompson wanted to know.

"Well, knowing Johnstone, I think he'll be very careful."

"What do you mean, careful?"

I was getting stiff so I stood up and moved around. "Jay Johnstone isn't one to gloat and kick a man when he's down, O.K.? But he has some bad feelings toward Dewey. I asked him one day—I worked with him when I was a rookie—I asked him why he didn't like Dewey. 'Course Johnstone had never said anything, ever. It was just the way he got real quiet when Dewey came around. And me being the new kid on the block, I had to know what was going on. Jay brushed me off at first. But I kept pestering him and he began to open up." I shook my head. "He hated Dewey Pringle like the Jews hated Hitler. And he's never changed his opinion."

I looked down at Thompson. "What happened tonight, Dave, you won't want to be talking about. The way Johnstone carried on, I mean. Just go back to work and, if it comes up, let it come from him."

"Why?" Thompson asked. "He's off now telling everybody about the kid." Dave motioned toward the cell.

"Not everybody," I corrected. "Only a few buddies who have been waiting for Pringle's chickens to come home to roost. Johnstone is a dignified, quiet cop. He has a sense of justice and tonight he enjoyed a little revenge. But he's a

private sort and I think we should respect that." I paused. "I
don't think it's right to take revenge. According to the Bible,
revenge belongs to God. But Johnstone knows that the Book
also says, 'Whatever you sow you will also reap.' Johnstone's
been waiting a long, long time for harvest."

»5«

The Monogrammed Handkerchief

Pete walked into the Division just then with a fistful of papers and perched his solid frame on the edge of my desk. "What's doin', Pumtwist?" He yawned and rubbed the back of his neck, then regarded Thompson, who was finally quiet.

"Just educating the youngster here in the ways of the world," I replied gravely.

"Pringle?" Pete asked.

Dave nodded.

"What's Johnstone got in his bonnet? He's buzzing about something with a couple of cronies."

"Had something to do with our new prisoner," I answered. "Something about her last name." Pete understood but did not reply. He looked tired, probably bored, like most of us, with inside duty.

"Finish the statistics report?" I asked.

In answer Pete exhaled, closed his eyes, and deliberately dropped his papers on the floor.

"Aw, whatsa matter with you, Blake?" I asked, delivering a punch to his upper arm. "Possibly you'd rather be out there patrolling those sin-sick streets, tracking down dangerous criminals, maybe getting yourself shot or killed, when you can be here with us? You want I should believe that?"

Thompson grinned. He liked Pete, too. "Yah, miss the street, Pete?"

Pete was warming to the scuffle. "Just want to be sure all the crooks and wrongdoers are found out and brought speedily to justice, is all," he exhorted. "You young rookies miss too much."

This observation brought a heated objection from Thompson, of course. We traded insults until we were all caught up in one of those unreasonably hilarious moods which can only be appreciated in the middle of the night. When the phone rang, I pulled out a trick I didn't often get to use. I jumped up as if to answer, then handed the receiver directly to Pete. Though caught off guard, Pete knew instantly what I was up to and tried to pass the instrument off to Thompson. Thompson was too fast for him, however, and darted out of reach. Pete was left to compose himself, clear his throat, hurl a whole fistful of pencils at both of us, and speak into the phone before the caller suspected police foolishness on the other end.

"Juvenile Division," Pete attempted, trying to sound solemn.

Thompson and I went into action. It required an ample amount of skill, bravery, and know-how to yank Pete's shirt out of his pants, pull off his shoes, roll down his socks (catching any tiny hairs we could), blow in his ears, and continually dodge his shots at us, but we managed. We were doubled over and Pete was in agony by the time he hung up.

"Palmquist," he thundered in a voice of fire and brimstone. "God will get you for that!" Thompson loved every minute.

Suddenly I straightened up. I had heard something. The brief mood vanished as I motioned for silence, listening intently for the sound again.

Kimberly!

She sounded funny, choked or something. Suicide leaped

into my mind. I checked the clock and realized Kimberly had been alone for almost an hour. I should have checked on her!

Fear and guilt washed over me in the few seconds it took to reach the door. I had closed it only enough to keep the light out of her eyes; for the second time that night I flung the door wide open. There was the pillow. And there—my heart lurched with relief—was the chair on its side, as I'd left it, with no feet dangling above it. But the choking sound was louder. I stuck my head further into the room.

Kimberly was still heaped up in her corner.

Pete had followed me to see what was happening in the cell. I decided I could handle Kimberly alone, so I waved him away just as he opened his mouth. "Later," I mouthed. For all our dashing around, we'd been remarkably quiet and Kimberly did not know we were there.

Pete frowned but backed out slowly. He was probably disappointed that he couldn't get a closer look at Dewey Pringle's daughter.

Looking down at Kimberly, I was touched again by her smallness and vulnerability. She sat in the corner, back to the door, arms around her knees, face between her legs, forehead resting on her locked hands. Her shoulders, draped all around with her long hair, heaved regularly, and she rocked slowly from side to side. She was completely possessed with grief.

Stretching my neck to peer around her hair-curtain, I saw the ample evidence of her tears. Her legs and feet glistened with moisture. Kimberly couldn't have slept very long. I almost wrung my hands. Why hadn't I checked on her?

Anger and pity rose inside me as I stood watching. I believed it was all Dewey's fault. Not his wife's fault, not his older daughters' fault, not Kimberly's fault. It was his fault. He had married, had children, then turned his back on them as he ran from woman to woman and bar to bar. As long as Kimberly stayed out of his way and didn't embarrass him, he didn't care what happened to her. Tonight she had gotten his attention, but what a price she had paid.

How often had she cried these tears of rage? I wondered when she had first begun to lose respect for the man she once must have worshiped, as young children all adore their daddies.

Why? What makes a man treat his child the way Dewey treated Kimberly? I had asked that question over and over, booking prostitutes or locating runaways. The fathers of those kids had a lot in common, and it occurred to me that Dewey Pringle embodied all the qualities I'd seen and despised in them. Dewey thought everyone saw him as tough and self-sufficient. But the big front he put up was transparent. His family and co-workers knew the real Dewey Pringle as a drunk, a poor excuse for a father and a husband, and probably one of the least competent Minneapolis policemen ever.

My neck and chest were growing hot and prickly and I could feel my rage growing. The longer I stood and watched that child, the more angry I became. Infantile though it was, I felt like hitting something with all my might.

I recognized this intensity of feeling from only one other time in my life. We'd received a family fight call; the husband had come home drunk and mean, and had begun kicking his wife and family around. One of the kids had managed to sneak to a phone to call us.

Five minutes after the call my partner and I walked into what looked like a war zone. Every piece of furniture was overturned, broken lamps lay on the floor, a kitchen cabinet had been torn off the wall, and chips of blue dishes were scattered like confetti. From corners of the large living-dining room came cries and moans. To my left, a boy of four or five years lay on the floor, blood oozing from his mouth. On my right, a nine- or ten-year-old girl sat on the floor, shaking violently and covering her head. Her legs had been cut. The mother lay against the backside of an overturned sofa, holding her stomach and wretching spasmodically. Even the small dog, a mixture of collie and I-didn't-know-what, limped toward us slowly, trying to wag his tail.

The terrible scene hit us in one sweeping view and my partner turned white.

"My God, my God, what happened here?" I exclaimed.

As though answering bodily, the drunken father swaggered into view through a hallway door. Surveying the destruction proudly—proudly!—he slurred, "Well, I guess I sure showed them who's boss around here!"

My eyes narrowed as my blood pressure climbed. A hot prickling began in my feet, crept up my legs, spread across my chest and onto the back of my neck.

The father then started toward us, strutting like a general—if a drunk can ever strut. I felt a hard ball in my palm. It was my fist and it tightened with every weaving step he took. He was three feet away when I slowly leaned back, bracing my feet, tensing every muscle, and forfeiting any remaining shred of self-control. I slammed my right arm forward, connecting his jaw with all the strength of my 230-pound frame. His feet left the floor for an instant, then the bulk of his body thudded heavily down.

I released a long breath. Reality crept back into my brain, gradually replacing the blind fury, and my first clear thought was for the three broken human beings around me. I had just flattened a man in full view of his family. In spite of their conditions, surely they loved him or felt some loyalty for him.

I had acted stupidly. I had done to that man what he had done to them. Worse, I had no excuse for doing what I did. I was an officer of the law, and I didn't believe in using violence to settle differences.

I glanced at my partner. He knew, as I knew, I never should have hit that man. Never. But Skip said nothing.

Quickly searching the faces of that little family, I apologized, and was grateful to see each one in turn smile weakly. Whatever their feelings, they'd forgiven me, and were grateful for immediate relief from the one who had threatened their lives.

The crisis over, Skip pulled his cuffs, easily snapped them on the man's wrists (more as a handle than a safety procedure), and directed him down the walk to our squad car. I waited inside, doing what I could to make the family comfortable until the Hennepin County Ambulance arrived. Then I said goodbye and turned to leave.

My thoughts were in turmoil over what I had done and I almost stumbled over that silly half-breed dog. He had apparently placed himself in the doorway so I could not get away without a friendly word for him. To this day, I believe God sent that fuzzy creature to my aid. There was complete trust in his eyes as I knelt and kissed his hurt leg. I told him how stupid I'd been and yet how angry I felt, then I wished him a speedy recovery. "You'll be back out there chasing squirrels in no time," I promised him.

Later, I tried to sort through my feelings. There was a place, I was sure, for what some call "righteous indignation." Human beings, especially policemen, though they encounter cruel and unfair circumstances over and over and over, still cannot allow themselves to become uncaring, unfeeling machines. That would destroy a God-given sensitivity to life. On the other hand, to allow righteous anger to be replaced by blinding, unreasoning wrath was wrong, too.

Adding the element of my natural hot temper complicated things, too. I wrestled with the answers. How should I feel? What would please the Lord? What should I do when my self-control began slipping away? They're hard questions, classic questions, questions which do not yet have answers. But I made a start, at least: I vowed never again to smash a man's jaw out of anger.

But here I stood, angrily watching Kimberly sobbing over cruel and unfair circumstances, feeling that same hard ball in my palm again and becoming aware of that same hot feeling invading my body. I remembered my vow and prayed for control. Then I thought of Dewey Pringle, who had permitted his daughter—no, *encouraged* her by his selfishness—to wreck her life in thirteen short years, and I trembled in anger. And then I recalled the Lord's promise to provide an escape with every temptation. "Lord, where's that escape?" I prayed. "I *want* to hate, I *want* to hurt him the way he's hurt her, I *want* to be angry!"

I was taking shallow, quick breaths in my little battle between right and wrong. Struggling, seething, I grabbed the chair and slammed it down with savage energy.

Too late I realized this horrible crashing was Kimberly's first clue that I was in the room with her.

She bodily left the floor about four inches. Not only was her face filled with stark terror at the sudden explosion near her ear, but the tears had rearranged much of her makeup in a dreadful pattern. I will carry to my grave that first image of wild-eyed shock as Kimberly's head snapped up to see what clamoring monster was after her. Mascara had painted long black stripes over her flushed cheeks and the luminous green eyeshadow had relocated itself, some near one temple and the rest between her eyes. Most of the lipstick had been transferred to my handkerchief during the earlier mopping up, but a bright tiny smear had escaped to highlight one eyebrow. Over it all, an intricate network of blond strands was plastered, veil-like, by her tears. It was difficult to sort the bumps and cuts from the paint.

At least she had stopped crying.

When her heart began beating again, she gave me a why-couldn't-you-have-just-said-hello look, and dug out my handkerchief, no longer white. But the more Kimberly wiped, the worse her face looked. I began to laugh. I didn't mean to but, like getting an attack of giggles in church, I was powerless to stop.

Kimberly stared at me. Then, in spite of herself, she laughed too. Soon we were howling. The laughter worked like an overload switch (or perhaps a "way of escape"?) to ease our abnormally high anger levels.

"Hey," Pete called, "you havin' a party or something?"

"Ah, yeah, sort of," I called back.

The interruption restored a degree of order and Kimberly went back to mopping. But only a few minutes had passed before a fresh supply of tears began spilling down her cheeks and then she was crying again, hard. Emotion flooded her as she stretched, face down, across the cell floor. Harder and harder she cried. Her fists pounded the tile and she cursed her father over and over. She was so overwhelmed I worried that she would have a convulsion.

During my months at the police academy I had learned how to disarm a criminal, fire accurately at a moving target, drive safely at high speeds, identify illegal drugs, and overtake a fugitive. Had I learned how to calm a hysterical little kid? I had not.

"Do something," Pete said after assessing the situation from the doorway. He looked at me and, so help me, had every assurance that I'd recall Section Six, Paragraph Fourteen or something, and simply apply the solution. Good old Pete. Always such great confidence in me.

"Like what, for instance?" I whispered loudly.

"It'll come to you," Pete whispered back. He winked and left.

I rejected the only official thought that came to mind, that of having her admitted to the hospital where she could be sedated. "Only as a last resort," I pledged both to myself and to the grieving form. Then an idea began to take shape.

It was unorthodox, and I had no guarantee that it would work, but we had little to lose.

My daughter, Julie, had worked up a real tantrum one day. She wasn't being impossible, she was just hurt that one of her true-blue, friends-forever neighbors wouldn't play with her. On that particular day Julie was operating with too little sleep and too many irritations, so the hassle with her friend was her breaking point.

She stormed into the house in a real state. I couldn't understand a single slobbered word of her explanation, but I realized Julie had never been this agitated before. Gayle was out so there was only one course to pursue: instinct.

I reached down, surrounded Julie with my long arms, and hoisted her to my lap. I hugged her and talked softly into her ear, saying that things would be better soon, and there were lots of people around who still loved her, and what if she flooded the whole kitchen with her tears? She quieted down immediately and snuggled up against me.

Pizza has always made things better for me, so I asked if she'd like to go out for some. Julie considered this. But, no, she'd really like some french fries instead. Off we went to the hamburger shop, and when we returned forty-five minutes later, she had forgotten the incident.

It may have been the early hour, my lack of experience, or an inadequate amount of gray matter operating in my brain. I don't know; my deductive reasoning told me only that if a plan worked once it might work twice. Professionalism not-withstanding, I eyed Kimberly and wondered if people ever run out of tears. Stepping to the right, I calculated my best vantage point. No, too slippery on that side. The racket was playing havoc with my hearing by this time. Two steps to the left. Kimberly was oblivious to everything but her own misery. Yes, the left would be best since my stronger arm would be on top of the situation—literally.

Target in focus, I drew a quick breath, flexed my arm and shoulder muscles while I stalled for enough time to gather my nerve, and...took the plunge. Cop and kid landed lopsided in the old chair, eight arms and legs paddling the air frantically to gain balance. I ascertained Kimberly to be in the general vicinity of my lap. If the ploy worked, it would have to be added to the Operations Manual.

The shock of this unexpected maneuver sedated Kimberly magically. I said words I don't recall—phrases said to infants and kittens and houseplants. And I smothered her into my chest. Each second that passed was drier and more quiet.

Something made me think of Pete just then. His head appearing at the door was becoming a habit. My premonition was right: Familiar footsteps echoed outside. I squirmed. But the look on his face when he peered in to behold his partner consoling a juvenile prostitute on his lap was worth my embarrassment. Pete was wholly unprepared for the scene. There was nothing for me to do but to shrug it off, as if I was accustomed to this sort of thing, but Pete couldn't utter a sound. At last he threw his hands into the air and retreated.

Kimberly had stopped crying. The fatherly approach had worked, and the time had come for me to be a cop again. I stood her on her feet, steadied her until she got used to her heel-less condition, and looked her straight in the eye. We had to talk about her arrest. "Kimberly," I said seriously, then paused. "Say, would you like to use the ladies room?"

I escorted her and waited outside the door. She knew I was there and probably found it awkward to attend to personal matters, but I had no choice. Others, taking advantage of the private moment, had tried to commit suicide, having secreted tiny weapons in their bodily orifices. Kimberly had been frisked briefly, but a matron would be called in if there was any suspicion that a search was necessary. While I had no such suspicion regarding Kimberly, it was only wise to be cautious.

The water went on, then off, there was the sound of splashing, and then it was quiet. Very quiet.

"Hey, Kim, what are you doing?" I yelled.

"You'll see," she answered.

"But will I like it?"

"Sure," she said indignantly. The door opened shortly and a scrubbed and shiny—though slightly battered—countenance presented itself. The hair had been pulled into a long pony tail and the brown eyes, though red-rimmed and swollen, sparkled in the light. Kimberly walked out, struggling with the broken shoe, but holding her head high and proud.

She retrieved the pink sweater and wrapped herself in it, then she looked up. "O.K., Officer (and this time it wasn't an obscenity), how do I look?"

I smiled. "You look fine, Kimberly, just fine."

»6«

A Hole in the Wall

Kimberly knew it was my move now, so she studied me as we walked back down the empty corridor to the Division. I held her future in my hands at that moment. Undoubtedly, she was not afraid of any legal consequences; few minor offenders are, for the law is relatively kind to youngsters under eighteen years of age, and they know it. But what probably frightened her was that her pimp would be furious with her, and that she'd have no access to drugs if she were locked up. Should she try to run? Or would sweet-talk work on this peculiar cop? She squinted, and her forehead creased with the effort of intense concentration.

I was studying Kimberly, too, considering my options. I could R and R her (reprimand and release), or I could jail her, or I could . . . oh, this was a tough occupation I'd chosen. Maybe it would be best if I . . . but, no, I couldn't . . . well, why not?

I opened the door to Juvenile, where Pete still sat, patiently minding the phone.

"Kimberly, would you like some french fries?" I asked. It suddenly occurred to me that my stomach had been trying to get my attention for some time.

Kimberly's eyes rounded in surprise. "Uh, sure," she gulped. From the look on her face, I could tell she had never heard of the french fry aspect of arrest. It made me chuckle.

"Heart of stone, head of iron . . ." intoned Pete sarcastically. I ignored him.

I could have taken a squad car but thought better of it. I wanted Kimberly to trust me and a police vehicle would not help my image at all. So I grabbed my keys from my desk and held the door for Kim.

It was a two-block walk to my own car, and on the way Kimberly perfected a step-tiptoe, step-tiptoe technique. I had been unable to locate any other shoes; they seemed not to flourish as abundantly as Official Pink Sweaters. I laughed when she had to negotiate a grate in the street and she turned up her nose at me. Too proud and tough to admit that she was still in some pain, she nevertheless eased herself into the car slowly and carefully, a small moan escaping her lips.

She rode in silence, watching the street life sharply. Once or twice, I felt sure she ducked, pretending to fidget with her shoe or something. I quickly eyeballed the sidewalks and doorways to see who Kim was avoiding, but I couldn't tell for sure.

When I had worked with Teen Challenge in New York for three years, I had learned how to find the best hamburger joints: Look for spotless, stainless steel kitchens, clean countertops, fresh swept floors, and comfortable booths—then go to one exactly the opposite. You have to have a little dirt to round out the flavor.

My favorite all-night hamburger shop in Minneapolis was perhaps the most exactly opposite of all.

"How'rya doin', Al!" cried a huge voice. Harry always sounded as though he couldn't believe his good fortune in having you as a customer. Politely he waited until Kimberly wasn't looking before sizing her up. An almost imperceptible shake of his head told me he knew instantly what was going on and couldn't believe how young she was.

Greasy apron and all, the waiter—who was also cook, busboy, dishwasher, and owner—ran around the end of the counter to take an utterly meaningless swipe at our table with a gray rag. He beamed down at Kimberly.

"French fries," she declared.

But I had seen the creatures which had gone on to their rewards by straying too near the grease vat. "Anything you have that isn't fried," I ordered.

"You cops are getting fussy," complained Harry. He disappeared through an opening and created a variety of noises which eventually resulted in our getting fed. It didn't matter what I ordered, actually, Harry always brought me chili. That was one item on the menu that I could eat any time of the day or night. I love it. Kimberly dug into the steaming fries only after dousing them liberally with ketchup.

At that time, I had been a cop for three years, with only nine months' experience in the Juvenile end. In many ways I was still a novice. We'd seen a sharp rise in juvenile crime in the late sixties and into the seventies, especially in Precinct #1 which included downtown Minneapolis, and I was eager to learn all I could. Some cities stuck to a strict policy of apprehending the criminal and meting out justice; others, Minneapolis among them, had begun to emphasize a preventive approach, encouraging rehabilitation and community awareness. In this atmosphere, we tried to trace juvenile criminal activity to its source. Sometimes we talked to the parents, sometimes we recommended a help program, sometimes we arrested a drug pusher and sometimes, rarely, we were led to a pimp.

Kimberly could help me. She was sharp, alert, and she knew the streets. To send her home would be to write her ticket back to Fifth and Hennepin, so I searched for an alternative, one that would keep her within my reach and out of trouble. First, however, she would have to learn to trust me. I looked at her as I picked up my cola. She might have been Julie in a few years: blond, a little bony and with the slightest hint of acne, same turned-up nose, same passion for french fries. But Kimberly was distant, locked up behind a wall that I couldn't climb, not without her help.

I stopped musing when I saw her lips moving and realized she was no longer chewing.

"... gonna happen to me when we get back to the police station?" she was asking.

I looked down to chase a drop of moisture on the glass. "Kim," abbreviating her name as an attempt at friendship, "let's not worry about your arrest just yet. Let's worry about how to put your life back together, all right?"

She smiled faintly, toying with her glass, too. After a long, thoughtful silence, she took one brick out of her wall. "You got any kids?" she asked.

"Yup," I answered. "Julie and Ricky. Julie's in first grade; Ricky is in a crib."

She smiled, then grew silent again. Something was on her mind and it was killing me. I waited. Suddenly Kim knocked out a whole corner of her wall. "I wish ... umm ... I wish I had a ... a ... dad like you."

There it was! She'd done it! I struggled with a lump in my throat and proceeded with caution.

Kim didn't struggle at all. She'd found more tears somewhere and they flowed freely down her cheeks and chin. Quickly she snatched the napkin and covered her face with it.

"Kim," I said, praying for words, "you'd be a terrible daughter."

She peeked out, startled, from her white shelter.

"You'd probably use up all the tissues in the house. We wouldn't dare to catch cold or sneeze. There wouldn't be any tissues left. You'd have them all piled up to the ceiling in your room."

Kim was caught between laughing, choking, and sobbing, and the result was wet and noisy. But the tears stopped. "I'm sorry I said ... I didn't mean ... oh, I don't know what I mean! Are you mad? I'm so stupid. ..."

I leaned far over the table. "Listen, kid. I can't be your father. But I can be one of the best friends you'll ever have, and I'd like that a whole lot. How 'bout it? Can we be friends?"

No answer. Her elbow was on the table and her hand shielded her face from view, so I couldn't tell what was going on in her mind. But there was a lot at stake. I still carried a badge, for one. *C'mon, Kim,* I urged silently. I reached over and grasped her wrist so she would look at me. "Kim, we may as well be friends. You can trust me, you know. You really can. And we can help each other." I let go of her. "By the way, my name is Al."

Unsmiling, Kim took a very deep breath. After several tortured minutes she'd made up her mind about me.

"O.K." It was obviously a big decision. Kim wasn't used to being vulnerable and she studied my face intently, as though willing me to reveal any deep, dark schemes I had planned for her.

"All right!" I exclaimed with a smile. "All right, then, friend, you'd better wipe the ketchup off your chin." As she did so, I yelled for Harry to bring us another round of Cokes. When Kim reached for hers, I stopped her. "Hold it. Wait just a minute, here." Then I picked my glass up, touched hers lightly, and proposed a toast. "To a long friendship between the crybaby kid and the wacky fuzz," I said somberly. "O.K., now drink."

"Tell me about home," I said as Kim finished the last of her fries.

"What about it?"

"Well, for starters, what kind of dad would you like?"

She looked out the window. "I don't know. If we didn't fight so much, it would be fun to go different places with him, I guess. Sometimes I think, 'If he really liked me, he'd spend some time with me.' You know? I have this girl friend and she has a really neat dad. They invite me over sometimes and we go out for hamburgers or something. I've never gone out for french fries, ever, with my dad. Did you know that? We don't do nothin' together. He doesn't listen to me." Kim paused. "He doesn't even yell very often. Only when I make him mad or get in his way. And then he loses it. He gets crazy and, well, you know."

"So you get even with him."

"What do you mean?"

"Kim, it's not hard to figure out. If being good doesn't get his attention, maybe being bad will. Prostitution is a dirty, rotten way of life and you are not, *were* not, in it for the money, were you? No! It was your way of getting back at your dad."

"That's not true!" she said.

"Isn't it? All right, let's talk about prostitution. Tell me about the johns. Are they nice to you? Do you respect them . . . after?"

She wrinkled her nose. "They're gross! Most of them have booze breath and they smell and sweat and I hate 'em! They're awful. Like animals. They give you this number about 'the little woman won't have anything to do with me,' and I think, 'It's no wonder, creep! Go take a bath and bring her some flowers, for a change.'" Kimberly paused. "I always worry about gettin' . . . catchin' VD, too. Every little sore makes me paranoid."

I pressed harder. "How about the money? How much did you make this week?"

"Five hundred. Maybe a little more."

"Where is it?"

She shot me a cold look. "I used it."

"All of it?"

"Yeah, all of it. Get off my back."

"Whatever happened to it, it's not making you rich, is it? And it won't. It never does. I never met a rich whore, Kim."

She was getting angry but I wasn't through. "You're on drugs, too, aren't you?"

"Who isn't?"

"Do you think about getting hooked? Sure you do. But you need 'em to help you go through with it, right? Because if you ever started to think about what you're doing, you wouldn't be able to do it, would you?"

Kim was on the verge of running. "Kim," I said very gently, "you are not a prostitute now. You don't ever have to go back. There are better ways to deal with your dad than throwing your life away just to hurt him. We're friends; you remember that. I'll help you but you have to face the truth."

I felt sure I was right. Now I knew why Kim had told me her name so easily. She had used me. She'd wanted her father to find out about her. She'd wanted to hurt him. There was no way she could realize all the dangers she was exposing herself to. She had simply wanted his attention.

Still, something told me there was more to it.

I paid the check and we left. The sky still was dark, but "tonight" had mysteriously become "last night," and a new day had begun.

Kimberly was looking ahead, too. "Al," she asked, "what is going to happen to me?"

"Well, Kim, what do you want to have happen?"

She paused. "I want to change. But I don't know if I can."

"Do you have a pimp, Kim?"

Her face became cold, stony, and a strange darkness came into her expression. She clammed up exactly as she had earlier. Even in the car, there was no mistaking the message.

"Why won't you tell me?" I was exasperated. Kim would talk about everything else, but the pimp issue she kept beyond my reach. Why? "Kim, you have to tell me if I'm going to help you," I pleaded. But she was a statue.

In months to come I would discover that girls typically

refused to talk about their pimps. Most claimed not to have them. Years after meeting Kimberly I saw how evasive and cunning prostitutes could be, not only about pimps but their entire lifestyles.

One midsummer day in 1978 I picked up a copy of our major Minneapolis newspaper, the *Tribune*, where I read the results of a prostitution survey done in town by a local youth agency. Most prostitutes denied having pimps, claimed the youth agency. Most girls freely chose their "occupations," it said. Hardly any violence was found to be associated with prostitution, their study showed.

It sounded official and most people probably believed what they read in that article. The night I talked to Kim I might have believed it, too. I was still pretty naive. But I'd gained enough experience by 1978 to know that something was out of whack. I was convinced either the youth agency had totally missed the mark or there was some biased reporting going on.

Up until then, the *Tribune* had been enthusiastic about police interest in the prostitution problem. In the Fall of 1977, when the "Minnesota Pipeline" was discovered, an operation where girls recruited in the Midwest were shipped off to work the streets of New York City, a *Tribune* reporter had accompanied my partner and me on investigative trips to the Big Apple. For months, occasional articles appeared in the *Tribune*, giving helpful advice to parents and kids on recognizing and avoiding the slick charm of the pimps.

But this new, "soft" story represented a drastic shift for the *Tribune*, completely different from hard fact reporting, and I couldn't figure it out.

As a cop, I had seen that most girls in prostitution actually do have pimps. Furthermore, I had witnessed the violence of that kind of life; often it was bizarre, cruel, revolting.

I sat reading that newspaper account and thought of the dozens of eight-by-ten, full-color police photographs, filed just a few feet away, picturing prostitutes who had been tortured, beaten, mutilated, and murdered. They were shocking pictures. Were they all figments of my imagination, then? No! Those girls were real. Most had been booked for prostitution at one time; most would have denied having a pimp, had they been asked; many were very young.

I reasoned with friends: If you were to study a criminal activity such as prostitution, how would you go about it? You would try a logical approach. Prostitution is against the law. Who deals directly with people who break the law? Policemen, of course. Therefore, it would be rational to hire experienced policemen to question the prostitutes for your survey, policemen who have been trained professionally in interrogation tactics. Average citizens do not know how best to study something that violates the law, nor should they be expected to know.

The youth agency sponsoring the survey failed to ask the police for help or even advice. They lined up about eighty girls and asked questions they wanted answered. The eighty girls gave answers they wanted to give.

I learned from several of the prostitutes they had been offered ten dollars to take part in the survey. So they agreed, only to lie whenever there was something to cover up. Their pimps ordered them to lie about pimping, to lie about how they got into prostitution, and to lie about the beatings and torture. If they had not lied, they would have been beaten or tortured.

At best, the young people who questioned the girls and submitted that report were underqualified for the assignment. At the time, it was hard to understand why the *Tribune* gave front page coverage to the story. Members of the Vice Squad requested that the *Tribune*'s police beat reporters at least be permitted to report the other side of the issue. The request was granted, but the resulting article appeared, not on the front page, but in the back of a Saturday paper.

I would learn why that happened and what prompted the one-sided coverage. But whatever the reasons, the night Kim entered my life I still had lots and lots to learn about prostitution.

My question about Kim's pimp lingered between us for a long time. She realized I would not drop the subject, yet she struggled with a painful conflict, a conflict I could not understand. I parked the car near the courthouse where Juvenile is housed, turned off the ignition, and sat perfectly still in the heavy silence. I was applying my I-can-hold-out-as-long-as-you-can treatment. Kim shifted and I saw the apprehension, the stark fear etched on her features. It baffled me. Surely she knew by now I would protect her.

She finally offered me her answer. Wordlessly, taking note of the street light, she turned around and leaned forward. Careful to protect her modesty, Kim inched her blouse partway up her back until I could see briefly the reason for her fear.

The answer was written all too clearly. Lots of ugly little marks branded her skin in tiny "U" shapes. Someone very strong had struck her very hard. Oh yes, Kimberly Pringle had a pimp, all right.

»7«

The Jesus People

I sucked in my breath at the sight Kim presented, and my anger rose once again. What made grown men beat kids up like this?

All my hows, whys, and wheres erupted at once but Kimberly had no desire to talk. She stepped out of the car, her shoulders pink-sweatered again, and step-tiptoed toward the courthouse. She was sure independent! I scrambled to catch up.

In the Division again, Kim eased herself into the most comfortable-looking chair—mine. We both wanted answers and since I would be going off duty in an hour I had to make a decision now.

"You said this is your first offense, right?"

She nodded.

"O.K., then, I can R and R you." I thought she would know what that meant but she frowned. "Reprimand and release," I explained. "I scold you, warn you, educate you, threaten you, take you home, and you quit prostituting." I smiled. "Simple."

"Home!" she protested, with an obscenity. "I'm not going home! My old man will kill me!"

She was probably right. "Well, I know some people who will put you up, but tomorrow night you'll have to go home. You're a juvenile and we have no choice, Kim."

59

She shrugged. "So, I go home. Billy will have me back on the street by. . . ." Her hand flew to her mouth when she realized what she had said, and the fear returned.

"Your pimp," I concluded softly. Kim looked around nervously, and when I asked where Billy lived, she became a terror-stricken mute.

I sighed. Her anxiety was unreasonable, especially here at the police station. Why couldn't she see that?

I left her briefly to scribble my "R and R" notation on the arrest report, gather my mail and messages together, tell Pete our immediate plans, and go to the phone, hoping I wouldn't disturb my friends John and Millie at this early hour.

"Did I wake you?" I asked first.

"Not unless I've been sleeping through my breakfast!" John said goodnaturedly. "What can we do for you, Al?"

"Do you have a bed open for a day or so? For a girl named Kim?"

"We sure do. Are you coming now?"

"If it's all right," I said. I thanked John, hung up the phone, and told Kim it was all arranged. She stood up and yawned.

The further we drove from downtown Minneapolis, the more Kim relaxed and the more disturbed I became. I told her it was silly to worry about her pimp now that she was in the safe hands of the law, but Kim wouldn't listen to me. My conviction grew that she knew something I did not.

I'd never given much thought to pimps. They were, I generalized, overdressed, fond of Cadillacs, enemies of the cops, and generally considered slime. That had been true in New York when I worked with Teen Challenge and it was true here in Minneapolis. Whether as a minister or as a cop, my goal had always been to help the girls out of prostitution and into a new life. Rather than asking questions about "the

Life" or their "main man," I spent my time getting them out of all that filth.

However, my ignorance was hurting the execution of my duties. Younger girls needed more than an alternative; they needed rescue. As long as this gap existed in my street education, I could not do my best to recover and protect these youngsters.

Kim had to help me. I must try again. Pulling the car onto the shoulder, I decided to ask the Lord for wisdom. As soon as the car had stopped, I bowed my head in prayer. I confess the prayer was calculated to get a reaction from Kim almost as much as to get an answer from God.

"What's going on?" she asked. She was on the brink of sleep. "Are you sick or anything?" The morning rush hour traffic surged past us.

"I'm praying," I said.

"You're what?"

"I have to know Billy's name and address. God knows it and you know it. I was hoping one of you would tell me, too."

Kim probably thought she was having a bad dream. "You're praying? Here in the middle of the freeway? You're nuts! Nuts, nuts, nuts!"

"I know. Will you tell me now?"

"Al...oh, how did I ever get mixed up with you?" She paused. "Al, I can't. Don't you see? I can't! I can't tell you! He'll beat me. He'll beat me, Al. Is that what you want?"

"He won't beat you if you tell me where he is, for Pete's sake! I'll go arrest him and put him in jail."

She shook her head. "He has ways of...Al, you don't know what you're asking. You can't stop Billy. I wish you could understand, but you just don't know him, Al! So just please leave me alone, *please*."

I was sorry to have made her cry yet another time, but it couldn't be helped. Taking both shoulders in my hands, I turned her so she had to look me in the eye. "Kim, listen to me. I will stop him. I have ways, too, and Billy doesn't know me either. But you must help me, Kim. You must tell me where he is."

She whimpered, "I wish I could believe you, but I'm so afraid. Oh, if only you really could get him off my back and out of my life. If only I could be safe again. But he. . . ."

"Kimberly!" I spoke sharply and gripped her shoulders firmly.

It worked. Like a doll whose string had been yanked, she rattled off Billy's address, phone number, and his license plate number. Even in the midst of her fear, Kim had a terrific memory.

I closed my eyes and breathed deeply (yes, and thanked the Lord, too!) before releasing her. At last I had something to go on.

We had nearly reached John and Millie's home when it occurred to Kim to ask about her new residence. She wanted to know what kind of place it was and whether she had to pay anything.

No, I said. It was run by some Christian people from a large church with a special youth ministry, and they didn't need Kim's money. "A few other girls stay there, too," I added, "most from the street, I think. They're all Christians."

Kim looked at me. "You say that word like everybody else is a heathen or somethin'. What do you think *I* am, anyway?"

I smiled. Thought she'd never ask. "According to the Bible, a Christian is someone who has placed his or her faith in the risen Lord Jesus Christ, Kim. I've found that not too many people have really done that. It has to be a very special decision, not a way of life that you're born into, like being born an American. Hasn't anyone ever told you that?"

Skeptically, she shook her head.

"Do you want to talk about it?" I asked.

"I don't want to get in with a bunch of fanatics, Al. You're

O.K., I guess. Weird, but O.K. But I've seen those Jesus freaks out on the streets at night, singing their gospel songs and banging their tambourines. If these guys are like that, I'll run away, I swear!"

"Really?"

"I'd rather go home and take my old man's beatings."

"Kim, what do you know about Jesus?"

She shrugged. "I went to Sunday school when I was a kid. My ma made me. All I remember was this big book with pictures. They had Jesus sittin' on a rock, holding little kids, with birds flying around. I thought it was dumb."

I nodded. "I think you're right. But that's not what He's really like, you know. Actually, He was a friend to a hooker."

"Come on!"

I laughed. "It's the truth! He had a group of friends who were like street people—they were called disciples—and one of His best friends was a prostitute. Well, an ex-prostitute. He forgave her and cleaned up her life. He can do that for you, too, Kimberly Pringle."

"I don't believe that."

"Do you believe that He was a real man?"

"Yeah, I guess so."

"Do you believe that He is also God, that He died on a cross and came back to life in three days?"

"I don't know. I've heard it before, but I never really thought about it. Do you believe that?"

"Yes. I believe everything the Bible says. And the Bible says He came to earth, He was beaten and tortured, He died, and He rose again. Anyone who can conquer the power of death can conquer anything else: sin, Satan, evil, even the future. And once we place our faith in God, we become His children and He becomes our Father." I softened my voice. "The best Father anyone ever had."

We had pulled up in front of John and Millie's house minutes earlier, and since I thought Kim had had enough for one day, I opened my door to take her in and introduce her. But she didn't move. "What's the matter? They're really nice people, Kim, I promise. Nothing bad will happen to you here."

"No, no, it's not that," she replied, a tiny trickle descending her cheek. "I just can't believe this." She laughed and cried in the same breath, then reached for the sad, limp monogrammed handkerchief in her sweater pocket.

"Can't believe what?"

"Oh, you big dope!"

"Thanks."

"I thought . . . when you said you would R and R me . . . that you wanted . . . a return favor, you know? I figured this would be your apartment and you would have . . . sex with me, right?" She blew her nose. "Instead . . . instead you bring me to a Jesus house! I can't believe it, that's all."

"But, Kim, you heard my phone call to John, asking if you could stay here."

She looked into my eyes for a long moment, then shook her head slowly.

"Mister," she said in a unique kind of street slang, "that trick's been used before."

My education had begun.

On our way up the walk, I thought I'd best set the record straight with Kimberly. "Look," I said, "you're a cute kid and you're my friend, but no thanks. Ever. I'm not interested. I don't want sex from you, and I don't want you to even think of me in that way. That's the way it's going to be from here on in. Got it?" Then I hugged her and said, "That's a friend hug, O.K.?"

"You're really in love with your wife, aren't you?" she asked.

"You betcha. Gayle's a super lady. Why?"

"It shows," she replied.

John was waiting at the door and ushered us into the big,

homey living room. Breakfast aromas filled the air, and soon the creator of those delicious fragrances appeared, carrying a tray.

"Al! It's good to see you again. How's Gayle? And those little ones? Growing like weeds, I imagine. And you must be Kim! We're really glad to have you, Kim."

An attack of shyness had overcome Kim and all she could manage was a smile.

Millie set the tray down beside me and continued her chatter. "Now, Al, we had some blueberry muffins left over from breakfast, and here's a cup of coffee. I brought milk for you, Kim . . . do you like milk? I just need a few more minutes to get your bed fixed up and then we'll tuck you right into it. Al, would you like scrambled eggs with your muffins? No? You probably just want to get home after working all night, you poor thing! Well, I'll hurry, then." And Millie bustled off up the stairs.

John and Millie were wonderful people. I smiled, knowing we'd done the right thing. This was exactly what Kim needed.

Kim refused any food. "I'm just so tired," she said, slipping off her shoe-and-a-half and curling up in a corner of the sofa. When I offered her a plump pillow, she grinned and took it.

"What happened to her shoe?" John asked. Kim's eyes were already closed.

"She's had a rough night," I replied evasively.

He took the hint and changed the subject. By the time I had finished two muffins, a cup of coffee, and half of Kim's milk, I was pretty sure Kim was asleep. "I really appreciate you taking her in like this, John. She needs a real home."

John lowered his voice, too. "She looks it, Al. She's in rough shape."

I looked over at Kim. "She's been told that she'll have to go home tomorrow. I wish her father would consider letting her stay longer. But he's not the type who'd think much of a

Jesus house. He's a hard man." Briefly, I told John about Kimberly's arrest, including our trip to Harry's and the "punishment" her father had administered. "Will you have Millie check on her bruises?" I asked. "I'll arrange for treatment if she needs it."

John nodded. "You know," he said thoughtfully, "I've heard some of the other girls here talk about their fathers. They say the same things, that their dads have no time for them, they don't go places together, they don't really talk. The only way they can get any attention is to make trouble. It's sad."

Millie came in then, still chattering merrily. "There, now, we're all ready for company. You just come with me . . . why, bless her heart, she's sound asleep! I hate to wake her, but she will be so much more comfortable in her room, you know. Come on, dear, your bed is ready. Can you just walk . . . there we are, that's fine." Millie looked over her shoulder. "I'm waking her just so she can go back to sleep again!" She shook her head. "Kim, sometimes life doesn't seem to make much sense, does it?"

"Hey," I called. "I'll check in later, O.K.?"

Kim turned and leaned over the railing. "Oh, I'm sorry," she said sleepily. "Thanks for . . . well, thanks." She looked at Millie. "Can he call me here?"

"Well, of course he can!"

"O.K., call me here, will ya, Al?"

"Tonight," I promised. "After I get some sleep, too." They left and I stood up. "John, thank Millie for me."

"Sure. Now, Al, I think you should at least ask Mr. Pringle about Kim's staying. We have room and he could always come by to see her. I'll pray that God will work it out, all right?"

I smiled and turned the doorknob. But John put his hand on my shoulder and bowed his head. He was a man of his word, literally. And a man of faith, I reflected, listening to his simple, trusting prayer that God would allow Kimberly to remain with them and that her father's heart would be changed. He even prayed for my safety driving home. "Amen," he said heartily.

I gripped his extended hand. "Thanks, John. Thanks a lot."

"We'll hear from you tonight," he said. "Go home and get some sleep!"

John has a rare kind of spirituality, I thought, walking to my car. It's simple yet strong, solid, unshakable. Mature, that was it. He studied the Bible constantly, but his Christianity did not stop there. He got involved, he cared, he even sacrificed for the sake of others.

A long, shiny Cadillac passed as I pulled into traffic, and a twinge of apprehension gripped me. I tried to shake it off. Kim was safe, I told myself. The fear she had of Billy was unreasonable. Even if he found her, which was almost impossible, pimps are afraid of cops. He'd leave her alone.

For twenty minutes, all the way home, I pondered. I considered. I argued. I thought. I deliberated.

Not until I'd stopped in my driveway and reached for the ignition key was the decision finally made: I had a promise to keep. Kim was not safe from Billy merely because she was away from him.

Suddenly, all that mattered was locking Billy up, and the fatigue I normally felt at that hour was gone. I threw the car into reverse and sped away.

»8«

"Dear God," Prayed Kim

It took only eight minutes to drive from my home to the address Kimberly had rattled off. It was a large house in the Kenwood area of Minneapolis, an area which had once boasted the well-to-do, class A families, but now revealed only the shells of their homes. The interiors had been divided into cramped apartments.

Parked in the drive was a car bearing the license plate number Kim had given me, and I breathed my second prayer of thanks that morning. That car at that address was like receiving a green light from heaven. It was a Cadillac—Billy must know his "profession" well—pink, with a white vinyl top. An enormous set of chrome horns, cattle-type horns, so help me, graced the hood.

I sat outside Billy the Pimp's pad wondering what to do next. I had found him, but now what? On duty, I would have called for a backup, but my personal car had no police radio, of course. I should have driven to the nearest pay phone and done just that, but the thought never entered my mind. God must protect the innocent because what I did alone then I'd never do alone today.

Quietly I got out of my car and walked over to Billy's car. Vice cops called them pimpmobiles. My hands placed on the hood told me the motor was still slightly warm. Billy had been home less than an hour. My heartbeat picked up.

69

Ignoring the rickety steps, I hopped noiselessly onto the porch, then crept to one side of the front door. No sounds nearby. I nudged the door. Another green light! It was unlocked and swung open to expose a long hallway. The floorboards creaked under my weight, giving me the jitters, but on I went, hunting for the right number.

Voices floated from a room at the end . . . that was it! I checked all around me. No one in sight. I hadn't been seen yet. Very slowly, I edged along the wall until I reached the door, then I drew my gun. My heart pounded fiercely. But there was no turning back, so I reached a shaky hand out and tried the knob. On TV, doors are always locked and cops are always slamming their bodies against them, shoulders first, and they crash down. My partner and I had to do that once, just once. In the first place, the door wouldn't fall down and we were embarrassed. And in the second place, my shoulder hurt for two weeks after that.

Maybe Billy was expecting Kim, I don't know. But the apartment door was unlocked, too. So I walked in, my heart up around my vocal chords.

Four girls sat at an old kitchen table where they'd been playing cards and counting lots of money. Their clothing . . . well, let's just say that collectively their garments would not have weighed four ounces. Part of the game's payoff lay in a little pile—"reds."

Billy the Pimp (obviously, for he matched Kim's description) sat on a sofa in the corner, fully dressed, measuring cocaine. He also matched the widely-held stereotype of a pimp. Owning a car like his probably forced him to maintain an image. He was black, small, and slim, and he wore a pink polyester three piece suit. A black hat sporting a long feather sat nearby, and his manicured fingers flaunted five or six large, flashy rings. Looking closer, I saw several earrings set into his earlobes.

The apartment was filthy. With one bathroom and one tiny bedroom, it was inadequate for two people, much less five. Pizza boxes, pop bottles, beer cans, and cigarette butts were strewn all about. The windows were dirty. Clothing lay in heaps on the furniture and the floor.

They weren't expecting company this morning, I could tell by the looks on their faces. All five sat, mouths gaping, gawking at me. It came to me that I was supposed to say something now. "Freeze!" the TV cop would have said after crashing through the door. But this cop couldn't remember the word. I only stood pointing my large gun whichever way I happened to look. Tension permeated the room. Something in my head kept trying to prompt me: "Freeze! Tell them to freeze!" But my scared brain could not come up with that word.

Finally I blurted out, "Hi, how are you all doing?" That had never, ever been said on TV just before an arrest. Probably never will be, either.

Billy almost choked. "Who the _____ are you!" he exploded.

"Officer Palmquist with the Minneapolis Police Department," I answered correctly, then waited for further questioning.

Billy knew his lines, though. He moved toward a corner table, and I rather suspected that whatever he had over there might hurt me. "Billy!" I yelled. "Don't move!" It was coming back to me. "Don't any of you move! Billy, come here—*slowly!*"

That's how he came, too. I told him to put his hands on top of his head. Staring at the gun barrel leveled at him, Billy obeyed meekly. I snatched my handcuffs and extended them to one of the hookers. "Cuff him," I ordered, and she did.

I had everyone sit on the floor in a corner of the kitchen. There I could watch them while I planned my next move. I'd never captured five criminals at once unless you count the poor old winos who never gave me any problems. How should I handle this?

Billy had no trouble deciding what to do, however. He lectured: Rotten pig cops, stupid fuzz who don't know a crook when they see one because they sure had the wrong dude here, police brutality, wait'll I get my lawyer, and on and on until I told him to shut up. He did not shut up, however. He would sue me, I was wasting my time here as well as his, we didn't do nothin' wrong, spit, stupid pig fuzz, spit.

It was impossible to think with all that racket, so I picked up a pair of dirty socks and walked toward Billy. "If you don't keep quiet," I declared, "I will cram these socks down your throat."

"Oh, man, you can't do that," Billy said, confident there was something legal covering this situation.

I moved closer, socks swinging. Some weapon, those dirty socks. Billy clamped his mouth shut, realizing that, oh, man, I could and would. After that he remained quiet but for some muttering.

My head cleared when the racket subsided and I did what I should have done before ever coming in—I phoned for help. It took only three minutes for them to screech to a halt outside the building, but while we waited I questioned the black man. "What lovely instrument did you use on Kim's back, Billy?"

The girls looked quickly at Billy, then at me, and then at Billy again. A trace of Kim's terror was reflected in their eyes . . . I wondered what their backs looked like.

Billy became more insolent and arrogant at the question, and he threw his head back to laugh. My flesh crawled to think what Kim might have gone through at the hands of this warped pimp. He turned his face in contempt of me, keeping his ugly secret to himself.

Billy went to jail. Advised by the Police Legal Department, I wrote on the report "aggravated assault" and "possession of drugs." The four girls were held in the Juvenile Detention Center.

With the paperwork finished by nine o'clock, I headed home for some sleep. My exhaustion finally caught up with me and it was hard to keep the faithful old car on the road, but I settled into bed with a great sense of satisfaction. Kim and the other girls were safe.

It seemed only minutes before Gayle came in to announce brightly, "It's two o'clock, honey." I dived under the pillow. I didn't want it to be two o'clock, not now or ever. I needed sleep. I deserved sleep!

Gayle repeated the time and opened the drapes to prove the fact with hot yellow sunshine. She had brought with her a nice lunch and acted as if she wanted me to eat it.

I felt I was entitled to one last protest before opening my eyes. Although my groaning and moaning drew a fair amount of sympathy, Gayle reminded me that I had to be back at work in one hour and there was nothing she could do about that.

I peered out from under the pillow. "You could come here, under my pillow, and give me a nice kiss," I suggested.

Gayle laughed. "Then I'd be kissing a pig in a blanket, wouldn't I? All right, but your ice cream is melting."

Pillows propped all around me, I ate lunch, Jenny coveting every bite. I told Gayle all about Kim and Billy the Pimp. Gayle's personality suits her very well as a policeman's wife. Quiet, easygoing, supportive, and a great listener, she was the perfect counterbalance to my excitable, impulsive, tempestuous nature. If she worried about the dangers of my occupation, she said nothing, though she reached for my hand when I described the encounter with Billy.

"Here, Jenny," I said to the seemingly starving collie. "You

73

can have the last bite of my ham sandwich if you'll quit sitting on my legs. Gayle, I think she's getting fat! She put my foot to sleep!"

"Well, if you wouldn't feed her ham sandwiches, she'd be fine," Gayle replied. "Anyway, it's time for you to get out of that bed and into the shower. I'm going to put Jenny on her chain. C'mon, girl, let's go outdoors now."

"I'm just going to let Kim know about Billy," I said, tossing aside the covers and reaching for the phone.

"You're going to be late for work," Gayle warned in a singsong voice.

"I'll hurry," I said, dialing so quickly that I messed up and had to start again. Millie answered. "How's Kim?" I asked.

"Oh, she's doing fine, I think. I'd let you talk to her but she just woke up and is soaking in a nice hot tub right now."

"That's O.K., I have to report in at three o'clock. Will you tell her that Billy—that's Kim's pimp—I mean, he *was* Kim's pimp—anyhow, he's in jail on about three felony counts, and I wanted her to know."

Millie was excited. "Oh, praise the Lord! God is so good! Kim would like to hear about it from you, though, Al; I'm sure she would. Did you say you have to go to work again this afternoon?"

"Yes, sometimes they schedule us with only eight hours between shifts."

"Oh, you poor thing. You must be worn out! But since you're working anyway, I was just thinking . . . would they allow you to stop by and see Kim, maybe have dinner with us? That way, you could tell her yourself. It would mean so much to her, and I don't mind if you eat and run."

I laughed. "Millie, you're always feeding me! Yes, I can work it out. Is six all right?"

"Six o'clock is fine, Al, just fine. Now I hope I don't spoil the surprise before you get here! Oh, God is so good! We'll see you in a little while, Al." In her excitement, Millie forgot to say goodbye, and I had to chuckle. She was pure gold.

I scrambled into the shower and soon headed out the door on the run. "Don't drive too fast," Gayle exhorted from her perch on the front porch, where she was watching Jenny wrestle with about half the neighborhood population, Julie and Ricky among them. She was probably right, I thought. I only had fifteen minutes to get to work.

"Daddy, Daddy, I want a hug," Julie shouted when she saw me, breaking out of the wriggling mob on our lawn and running toward me.

"Daddy, Daddy, wanna hug," imitated Ricky. He tried to run also, but did not have quite the dexterity of his older sister yet.

"I can't now, kids," I called breathlessly over my shoulder. "I'm late for work. I'll hug you when I get home." They would be in bed by then, but what else could I say?

Julie stopped running and began to cry. "I want my daddy, I want a hug from my daddy!"

Gayle will take care of them, I thought, waving from the car as I pulled away. Gayle was a good mother. She'd explain that I had to hurry and that I could play with them tomorrow.

My head swam with the events of the past twelve hours. Meeting Kim and taking my first few steps into the corrupt world from which she had come was significant to me. I felt that I was on the precipice of a vile, filthy pit, a pit which had always existed but which I'd been able to ignore. Now, because of what I was seeing in the Juvenile Division, especially in Kimberly Pringle's case, the pit had my attention.

Kim knew more than she had yet revealed. Given time, protection, and genuine trust, she could coach me, train me in the workings of that foul pit. It seemed to me she'd be the perfect candidate for the job. On one hand, she had likely seen enough in her three months with Billy to know what she was talking about. And on the other, she had not been into prostitution long enough to disfigure the rest of her life. There would always be scars, like those she would forever carry on her back, but they would not cripple her.

I wiped away a trickle of perspiration. This would not be a pleasant task, but I was eager to get started. If that was what it would take to help kids, that was what I would give. My work at Teen Challenge in New York had whetted my appetite, setting the direction that I would probably pursue for the rest of my life, that of reaching and helping street kids.

There was another reason for my fervor. A little over two months earlier I had been approached by both the Chief of Police and the Mayor to explore the possibility of opening a home for dopers and street kids in Minneapolis. In fact, I had been transferred to Juvenile Division as a part of that effort, to learn the new laws about juveniles and to observe how this very specialized law enforcement unit worked.

The challenge of the assignment was colossal, and I let my reservations be known. But it was interesting and it was an order. Besides, like most cops, I hate to fail. So Kimberly's arrival in the picture was timely.

As usual, there were no parking places near the courthouse, so I was hot and sweaty after running several blocks from my parked car to the Division. The Lieutenant was reading roll call and I dropped into the chair Pete had held for me only seconds before my name was called.

"What about Pringle's kid?" Pete whispered after I had caught my breath.

I gave him the highlights in low tones, as I didn't want the Lieutenant to tell me to be quiet. Pete grinned at the part about Billy, but then proclaimed me an idiot to have gone into the apartment alone. He was right, but I took exception to being labeled an idiot and jabbed him in the ribs.

"I bet she doesn't stay at your Jesus house, though," Pete speculated.

I frowned at him. This was a new thought, one I did not like at all. I'd considered the possibility that her father may not let her stay, but I had not considered that she might want to leave. Furthermore, I was irritated that I hadn't thought of it first.

About that time, the Lieutenant was reviewing the previous day's activities and he mentioned Billy's arrest. As was the tradition over any achievement, mine was recognized with a few cheers and encouraging remarks from the rest of the officers. That made me feel a little better, and when the Lieutenant asked to see me after roll call, I gave Pete a conceited snub.

Then we were assigned cases and I was pleased to receive only one: church vandalism by a gang of kids. Probably wouldn't take too long, leaving me plenty of time with John and Millie and Kim.

We were dismissed and I walked forward, straight and tall. "Palmquist," the Lieutenant began. He had lowered his voice so the other guys couldn't overhear him but there was no mistaking his tone. I was in trouble.

"Officer Palmquist. . . ." He paused, then continued, "I've heard of some dumb stunts in my time, but the manner in which you conducted the arrest of Billy DuMont was not only stupid and dangerous and ignorant, but unprofessional. Maybe you think it was brave. Or maybe you think since everything turned out all right, why make a fuss? Well, I'll tell you why, Palmquist. If it had *not* turned out all right, if just one thing had gone wrong, I'd be short one officer this afternoon! A wife and what? two kids? A wife and two kids would be without a husband or father this afternoon. And what if some cocky youngster who has just become an officer with us got it in his head to outdo you, Palmquist? He could get blown away! And do you know who would be responsible, Palmquist?"

He went on until I was reduced to a pile of dust on the floor. Finally he dismissed me after reminding me I was a good officer who had made a mistake, not to do it again, and not to go around bragging about it.

Pete was waiting outside the door and guessed, from the look on my face, what had happened with the Lieutenant. "Got on you, huh?" We walked down the hall in silence. Finally Pete placed a comforting hand on my back. "Pumtwist," he said philosophically, "look at it this way: Right now this city has one less pimp and five less prostitutes because of you. In my book, any win is still a win, baby! Heck, I'm jealous . . . how often does a guy get a chance to be a hero? Hey, do you wanna meet somewhere for hamburgers?"

I told Pete about my plans to see Kim.

"A home-cooked meal? You dog!" Pete teased. "Well, catch you later, then. Boy, I'm glad we don't have inside duty tonight! If you get a chance, why don't you drop by Harry's joint around ten? I'll need a chili fix about then!"

I chuckled and promised to try. Pete had a way of picking me up, that was sure.

We each grabbed a squad car and headed out. Pete was right. It felt good to have a steering wheel in hand again. With an eye on the clock, I patrolled for about an hour, then aimed the black-and-white out south, hoping all the citizens would behave themselves tonight because I wanted to enjoy a complete meal and talk to Kim. If she had not run away. I pressed down on the accelerator.

Kim was curled up on the same sofa she'd fallen asleep on less than twelve hours earlier. I recognized the book she was reading as Dave Wilkerson's *The Cross and the Switchblade*, but Kim was a different girl. Her hair was bouncy, she was fully clothed in blue jeans and a light shirt, her makeup, though still a bit heavy for her years, was clean and in all the right places, and she looked fresh and rested.

Apparently Millie had kept me and my news a secret, for Kim looked up, surprised. "I thought you were gonna call me," she said.

"O.K., I will," I responded. Cupping my hands around my mouth I yelled, "Kim! Kimberly Pringle! This is old Big Mouth Al calling!"

She laughed and got up from the sofa. As she walked, I noticed a slight limp and looked quickly at Millie. Millie shushed me with a quick shake of her head, so I said nothing to Kim, who was talking about the "super neat story" she was reading. I listened for several minutes, wondering at the transformation in this girl. She belonged here. If only we could make Dewey see that.

At last Kim paused for air. I seized the opportunity to say I knew all about the book and Dave Wilkerson and Teen Challenge.

Kim looked skeptical.

"I should know, Kim. I worked with Dave and his brother, Don, in New York for several years."

"No kidding?" she asked. "You really know that cat?"

Her remark prompted me to recall a few entertaining tales from those days, such as the time a generous soul donated a truckload of baked beans. We served beans for breakfast, lunch, and dinner every day.

I was pleased to see Kim so impressed with the "super neat story" of the New York ministry to street people and hurting kids. Maybe, I thought, that means Pete is wrong. Maybe Kim won't run away. She seemed to have a special sensitivity to spiritual matters which heartened me.

She certainly did not sound like someone who wanted to run away. She talked about her new friends: Her friend Jill's clothes just fit her, and everyone shared their makeup with her, and there was a garden out back where she'd picked peas for supper. Leaning closer, she said softly, "They're all kind of religious, like you said, but not freaky. Just, well, goody-goody. But they're O.K. They made me feel at home already."

Carrying something that looked yummy, Millie called everyone to dinner. Everything about this place is big, I thought—big dining room, big homemade table, big family and big hearts. We observed the custom Millie and John had begun at the time of their marriage twenty-six years previously, that of standing behind our chairs until each one present had offered a short prayer of thanks.

An idea popped into my head. I made it a practice to keep a tiny transcriber in my pocket for interviewing suspects and witnesses or for taking testimony. If Kim came to know the Lord someday, she might find it really meaningful to have a record of this prayer, her first, undoubtedly, in many years. When everyone bowed their heads, I slipped the instrument out of my pocket and behind my back. When Kim's turn came, I nudged the "on" button.

"God," began Kim, "I have never prayed before but I think You're around here. I'd like to know more about You, God, if You could work it out. Could You help Al, too, God, with the big job he has to do? Oh, yeah, thanks for this food. Amen."

She was the last to pray—John had arranged the order thoughtfully so she would have some extra time to get used to the idea—and I quickly stuffed the recorder into my pocket again before someone caught me. Scraping and scrambling, then, we seated ourselves to begin the huge meal. Passing bowls and platters, John said, "Kim, that was a nice prayer. And God will answer the part about wanting to know Him because He wants us even more than we want Him." Then John added with a twinkle, "And part of your prayer has already been answered."

80

Kim put down her fork and looked at me. She was a smart kid. "Is he in jail?" she asked, scarcely breathing.

I grinned. "And the girls are O.K. Since eight this morning."

Millie was ready to explode. "Oh, I was so afraid I'd give away the secret! I had to bite my tongue all afternoon. I knew you'd want to ask so many questions, Kim, and since Al was able to come for dinner...I tried so hard not to let on!"

"You knew all this time and didn't tell me?" Kim interrupted, without anger. "Oh, I can't believe it! How did you do it so fast? What happened? Were there four girls?"

"Kim," I said, "I'll tell you but you're holding up the potato salad."

Between bites I told the whole story, hindered occasionally by her questions.

"Well," she said authoritatively when I had finished, "you did a few things wrong. For one thing, there was a loaded gun taped under that kitchen table. One of the girls could easily have shot you right in the head. They're loyal to Billy."

Millie gasped, choking on her meatloaf. When John had administered a glass of water and she was breathing freely once more, Kim resumed. "Second, there are thousands of dollars' worth of drugs hidden in the apartment and you should have searched the place before Billy's friends had the chance to lift 'em. And third, you should have stuffed the dirty socks in Billy's mouth!"

Fighting crime was hard on the ego, I decided. This was the third scolding I had taken for going to the trouble of risking my life to put that pimp away. Maybe I should look into another line of work.

"Why did Billy keep such a big drug supply?" I asked. "Was he pushing, too?"

Pimps like Billy, Kim said, made most of their money off drugs, not prostitution. Some girls were known as "coke girls"—they were specialists in the use of cocaine. The cost for being with a "coke girl" could be very high, maybe $2,500, but some men believed she could solve their impotency problem so were willing to pay it.

My mind detoured for an instant: That would explain why some prostitutes wanted their profession legalized. Certain women in our city, addressing a number of citizens' groups, had been quite vocal about the "unfair laws" concerning prostitution. Legalized prostitution would certainly increase the number of customers, but most hookers despised their trade, and I could never understand why they would go to the trouble of promoting it. Why would they want more johns when their pimps claimed most of the take? However, if they made lots more money off each contact by selling drugs, too, they would likely consider it an equitable trade for them and for their pimps. Besides, the guys in Vice had talked about finding a few grains of cocaine on some of the hookers they'd arrested. Kim could be right.

Some folks would be offended at this sort of talk over dinner—or anytime—but Millie and John were accustomed to it as a by-product of their ministry. Nevertheless, Millie steered the conversation toward more pleasant things because she "had the responsibility of turning her street urchins into young ladies."

Millie invited Jill to share her testimony. "I'm wearing her clothes," Kim reminded me in a loud whisper.

Jill said she never knew who her parents were. She decided, at ten years of age, to run away from her foster home. She lived on the street, making most of her money carrying drugs for pushers since the cops weren't likely to suspect a child. When she got a little older she peddled her own drugs and prostituted herself.

(I couldn't keep from smiling at Millie's expression; apparently she had hoped Jill would leave out that part.)

Because she would not allow pimps to control her, Jill was beaten so often her body could no longer be sold. One night she wandered into the Jesus People church downtown where she heard how Christ could change her life. After the meeting, one of the pastors prayed with her and she found the Lord. That's where she met John and Millie, who had brought her to this Jesus House three weeks ago.

The four other girls told similar stories. Kim listened intently. John caught my eye and flashed me a knowing grin—won't be long before the Lord gets hold of Kim, that grin said.

Millie's strawberry shortcake nearly finished me off. "I won't be able to apprehend any crooks tonight," I groaned. But I finished the last delicious bite.

That did not appear to disturb Millie in the slightest. She sent us "menfolk" to the living room while the ladies—all but Kim since it was her first night and she didn't have to help, they said, but wait until she saw what she had to do tomorrow!—cleared the table and loaded the big dishwasher. They were rushing to get to a Bible study then, but I stopped Kim long enough to tell her I would see her later, wondering if she would say anything about going home.

"Later," she echoed lightly, banging the door in her haste.

"John," I said with mock seriousness, "I can see that this is all wrong for Kim. She's not happy here and her heart is still back in the streets."

John laughed. "She has some rough edges but she fits into our little family just fine. She is starved for affection, though. Right now she is too proud to say so, but she loves to have Millie hug her. Does Kim have a mother?"

I told John as much as I knew about Dewey Pringle and his former wife, including the rumors.

He shook his head. "Well, it's time to talk to him, you know," he said. "I think it would go better for Kim if you talked to Mr. Pringle face to face and told him how well she is adjusting to us. Let him know he's welcome to come see her whenever he likes."

I nodded and sighed. "I thought I would go by his house now to see if he's there." Much depended on that visit and I was nervous about it.

"I've seen a lot of publicity lately on men being tough—this 'macho' thing, they call it," John said. "Not that it's anything new for a man to want to be invincible, I guess. But the idea is being pushed so hard that men are getting sucked in by it." He sipped coffee from the steaming mug he had carried into the living room.

"There was something on Channel 2 just last night about it," John went on enthusiastically. "They were talking to a doctor about the effects of machismo on us men."

"What'd they say about it?" I asked.

"That it was killing us."

"Killing us? How do they figure?"

"Stress," John replied. "Had something to do with the conflict we create in our bodies when we believe we're supposed to be tough, but then we experience the gentle, tender feelings that are natural to us. If the feelings don't seem to fit the macho image, we bury them. After awhile, this doctor said, we've built up a tremendous strain which can cause ulcers, nerve problems, or even heart attacks."

I felt vaguely uneasy. "John, why do I feel that I'm getting a lecture?"

"Oh, I'm sorry, Al! I didn't mean . . . well, maybe I did. Truth is, that doctor said some occupations tend to attract the macho type of guy, and law enforcement was one he named."

"John, my ego has had a very bad day," I said, covering my heart.

He laughed. "Now, don't get your nose out of joint! You're a good friend and I'm not tryin' to bug you. But when I think of all the work you're doing right now I don't see how you have time for Gayle or your kids, not to mention the Lord. And here you are, trying to set up a home for neglected kids." John put down his coffee cup. "There," he said, "end of sermon! By the way, how *is* that project coming?"

I lay my head far back on the sofa, moaning and pretending to extract arrows from my chest. John chuckled. "Now you know how your parishioners felt!" he said, referring to my years as a pastor.

"Well," I said in answer to his question, "a few churches have offered to put us in their budgets; I imagine the total comes to about $1,200 a month. And I am keeping my eyes open for a home. Other than that, I'm just learning to be a Juvenile Officer."

Millie came in from driving the girls to their Bible study and I turned the conversation to her. "That limp of Kim's . . . does she need to see a doctor, Millie?"

"Oh, I don't think so," she replied. "She's bound to be pretty stiff for a day or two—that was quite a licking she took. Let's see if it takes care of itself by then." Millie, too, was taking Kim's future for granted. "A good dose of T.L.C. will put her right!" Millie said cheerfully. "Anyway, Kim's a spunky girl, not one to be looking for sympathy."

I smiled. "That's the truth!" It was time to go and I thanked Millie for the meal as I rose. John followed me to the door as always, and again offered prayer, this time for my visit with Dewey.

Heading for Dewey's place, I mulled over what John had said. The most painful image was of Ricky and Julie running toward me for a hug. How many other times had I been too busy for them? I wondered. And Gayle. She always tried to make time to listen to my gab, but had I overlooked her needs? Of all the blasts I'd suffered today, this was the worst. Had I really neglected my own family?

Next I thought of Dewey. I'd been quick to accuse him of being rude, callous, self-centered, a bully and a bigmouth; and unquestionably he was all that and more. But (and oh, these were unwelcome thoughts!) did I despise in Dewey some of the same tendencies that I struggled with: my anger, my drive to be best, my accomplishments?

John . . . now, John was a man to admire. A man of humility, yet strength. I looked up to him, respected him. John was secure enough in himself and his God to be able to love and care for others; his ego did not need constant feeding, maintaining, bolstering. He was free. Free to serve and free to feel.

"Oh, God," I prayed at last, loosening my tense grip on the steering wheel, "I'm guilty. I have been selfish, haven't I? And quick to anger. And too busy for my family and all the rest. Forgive me, Father, and show me how to change, 'cause I'll never be able to do it by myself. And Lord, please help me to love Dewey Pringle as You do no matter how I feel."

I was drained. Coupled with too little sleep, too much food, too many rebukes, and the severe, emotional combat the Lord and I had just resolved was the impending visit with Dewey. I pulled to the curb and looked at the house.

"I sure could use some sleep," I reminded the Lord. "You'd better go first." Then I took a deep breath and got out of the squad car, trying to anticipate what lay ahead. My worry was that he would listen to my little spiel, say nothing, then show up later at the Jesus House demanding that Kim go home. Dewey always seemed to be off somewhere in his own world so that I never knew what he was really thinking.

Dewey answered my knock and invited me in. He had been drinking but was not drunk. Quickly I laid it all out: Kim; Billy the Pimp; John, Millie, and the Jesus House; my conviction that his daughter be allowed to remain at the Jesus People house awhile.

He listened politely, as I had feared, nodding from time to time. But when I finished he sighed. "Well, that _____ kid never was any good," he said. "I guess maybe she should stay with those people in that house. I've tried to do something with her for years. She's just no good, no good." He lapsed into a long silence.

Much as I differed with Dewey, I was incapable of anger at that moment. He had agreed. Kim could stay! And I was certain he would stand by his decision.

"Do you want a drink, Al?" he asked.

"No, no thanks. But I wouldn't turn down a soft drink." Dewey shrugged. "Help yourself."

We sat for over an hour talking. That is, Dewey talked. He didn't make a lot of sense but that was all right; I could listen just the same. It was close to nine when I looked at my watch. I told Dewey I had not done much for the city yet and had better get cracking on my church damage case.

Outdoors, I breathed the fresh evening air and felt a twinge of pity for Dewey. He was such a mess, and his home reflected the disorder of his life. Every ashtray in the house was spilling over, empty beer cans lay everywhere, and the kitchen was in shambles, hidden under dirty dishes and spoiled food. Even the rug was stained and dirty . . . lots of booze had been spilled in that house.

»9«

Kim's New Father

"You mean you're still talking to me?" John asked in surprise.

I pulled the phone cord out of Jenny's mouth and nudged her out of the kitchen with my knee. "John," I answered, "I wanted you to be the first to know that I have dirt under my nails from playing trucks with Ricky; I have grease on my pants from riding bikes with Julie; I have wood ticks in my hair from running Jenny through the park; and I'm sweaty from playing tennis with Gayle. How'm I doing so far?"

"Is that the truth?"

"Nothing but," I answered. "I may die from exhaustion but never from stress."

"Al, I'm impressed. I have only one thing to say to you."

"What's that?"

"You need a shower."

We laughed and then I said seriously, "You said some things yesterday I needed to hear, John. I didn't know it then, but I did. Thanks."

"Oh, I get to meddling now and then, Al. But I threw away much of my youth and I guess I've tried to make up for it ever since by helping other youngsters avoid the mistakes I made. Millie and I had no children of our own so I kind of pick on you. And our girls, of course.

"Say," he added, "it seems to me you called yesterday

about this time. You wouldn't be fishing for another dinner invitation, now would you?"

"No, not tonight, John. I can only go so long without chili, you know. Actually I called with some good news. Dewey told me last night that Kim could stay with you folks. You must have been praying."

"Well, Kimberly doesn't know this yet—she's still out shopping with Millie and the girls—but I met Mr. Pringle about an hour ago."

Oh, no, I thought immediately. *He's gone back on his word after all.*

"Where did you meet him? Did he want Kim to come home? He didn't get tough with you, did he?"

"Calm down, Al," John laughed. "He was fine. He just stopped by with some of Kim's clothes, which was quite considerate, I thought. I'm sure she had not phoned to ask for them.

"He was either nervous or embarrassed—I couldn't tell which—because he set the suitcase down and just stood at the door. Wouldn't even wait for a cup of coffee. Said he had to get back to work. Anyway, he looked the house over for a minute and shuffled his feet, then reached into his pocket and pulled out a twenty-dollar bill. He told me to get Kim whatever she needed. Then he left. I felt that he was trying to thank us in the only way he knew."

John paused, then said, "I wish he had asked to see Kim, even though she was out. At least I could have told Kim her father had asked about her. But he did do something responsible, and that should mean something to Kim."

"Well, that's a relief," I said. "Looks as though Kim's immediate future is settled, then. Did he say he would come back?"

"Hard to tell. When I invited him, he had a distant sort of look and only nodded his head. Maybe he'll come for dinner one day. I feel sorry for the man, Al. He has no family, his girls became prostitutes, and he's probably an alcoholic. Without the Lord, the only thing he can hang onto is his image, such as it is."

"By the way, John," I said, "Gayle and I have discussed it and we'd like to help with Kim's support, too. Should we just send you our checks?"

"Nope. The church has us in their home mission budget and we are receiving enough to be quite comfortable. It is kind of you to offer—you know that—but any extra money you can scrape together should go into your project." Then John laughed, "Al, if I'm so smart, how come I just turned down your money?"

"I never said you were smart, John, only that you were right. Well, I've got to get to work. Oh, wait . . . would you tell Kim I need to talk to her soon about Billy's trial? I'll call her."

"Is it really necessary that she testify?" John asked.

"Critical. I know how you feel but we can't put Billy away without her testimony. Gives us something else to pray about, doesn't it?"

Gayle came in with the mail as I hung up. "Hon, we have two checks for the project house. If this keeps up, we'll be able to buy one in about thirty years. Isn't that great?"

I smiled. It was hard not to get discouraged sometimes. The word was getting around, but more people called us to get help for their kids than to offer money. The need outweighed the resources ten to one; I couldn't see how the dream would ever become a reality.

"Oh, come on, now," Gayle said, putting her arms around me. "It's too late to turn back and too early to quit. Just keep lining up church meetings and it will work out, you'll see."

Leaning down, I returned her embrace and added a tender kiss. Unfortunately, Julie and Ricky, with their terrific sense of timing, chose that moment to say goodbye, also.

"Daddy, Daddy, I want a hug! Hug me too, Daddy! Wanna

hug, Daddy!" Jenny even gave a few barks to let me know my wife and I were no longer alone. I wasn't crazy about the idea of their tugging on my clothes, either, knowing how many million things their hands had touched today. (Actually, I had taken a shower before calling John, and I thought the wood ticks had all been found.) But I kneeled on the floor to child height and said goodbye in true father fashion.

The scene I left today was much happier than yesterday's, I reflected as I departed for work. John may have done me the biggest favor of my life.

But my thoughts were heavy when I turned them toward my assignment. We needed to start a home, there was no doubt of that. With all the experience and training I'd had in New York working under Dave and Don Wilkerson, I was a natural candidate, I suppose. I remembered Mayor Charles Stenvig calling me into his office one day.

"Al," he'd growled. (I liked Charlie; he was tough and firm but had a soft heart for people.) "Al, we need a place for the street kids to go and get straightened out. They're not getting help from the penal system; they may learn how to become better thieves and pushers in prison, but they are not coming out of jail as useful citizens. Even the ones who want to go straight don't have a chance. They go back to their old friends, old environment, old life, and before they know it, they're doing dope again.

"It's the same with the first-time offenders; if they show any signs of wanting to make it, they've got to have help.

"Now, this Teen Challenge outfit, they had a high cure rate, didn't they?"

I had told him it varied but was well over seventy-five percent.

"All right, if we could do something like that here, we could at least give those youngsters who want it the help they need. And we want you to try it. We'll stick you over in Juvenile so you can find out what you're up against. You'll

92

have to know the laws. And then I'll give you some free advice: Stay away from government funding. Too much red tape. And every time a program changes in Washington, you end up with some new regulation. All you'll need here, with a simple nonprofit status, is a city license."

He'd leaned back in his chair and tapped his desk for a second. "Tell you what, preacher... you trust God for the money and then hustle everybody you can."

The Chief of Police at that time, Gordy Johnson, was all for it. He'd do all he could to help, he said. Gordy shot straight from the hip, too, and I knew he meant it. When I promised to think about it, Gordy walked out the door with me.

"I don't know, Chief," I had said. "I'm a cop. Can't you just see some bleary-eyed drug addict, fresh off a fix, come draggin' up to me saying, 'Uh, Mr. Policeman, do you think you could help me get off drugs and find Jesus Christ, 'cause I really want to get my life straightened out, Mr. Policeman'?" I laughed. "How many kids do you suppose will do that? This isn't New York. I just don't know."

But Gordy wouldn't let me talk myself out of it. "Try it, Al. It's an assignment; you'll get your salary no matter what happens. Can't hurt to try." He was an honest man but he'd used trickery on me that day. He knew once I'd started I wouldn't be able to let go.

I sighed. I'd have sooner given up chili than let those men down. Not to mention the kids we wanted to help. But where was I going to get the money? *Where?* Buying a house, which looked utterly impossible right now, was only the beginning: We'd have to hire a staff, pay insurance fees and licensing fees, install a phone (I couldn't live without a phone), buy food and sheets and towels and other necessities... it was just too much.

But Sunday morning came and I found myself behind the pulpit in a little church, talking as if the project could actually be done. And then Sunday night came and there I was in another church, behaving like I believed we could do it. Together, I reminded the folks. No one has to do it alone, I said, but the work cannot be done without each one doing his or her part. Then we sang a hymn and people asked questions and I was handed another check. Not large, but big enough to keep me hanging on.

"Gayle," I said later, sprawled in front of the television. Jenny had taken it upon herself to share my popcorn. "How are we gonna know when it's time to raise the white flag? I mean, sooner or later we'll have to give up, won't we? They just don't sell houses for two or three thousand dollars anymore."

Gayle gave me one of her pearls of wisdom. "When the money stops coming in. You can give up just as soon as people stop believing in what we're doing." Then she became very mysterious. "There was a call for you . . . a Miss Kimberly Pringle. She sounded excited about something."

I leaped to the phone. "It's late, Al," Gayle objected, then let me go.

I've never been quite sure of everything that transpired after I dialed John and Millie's phone number. To begin with, a loud hum started as soon as they picked up the receiver. We shouted the entire conversation.

"Hello, Millie?" I yelled.

"Hello? Hello?" I heard.

"Is this Millie?"

"No. Can you hear me?" the feminine voice inquired.

"Yes, if you'll just speak up. . . ."

"Well, this isn't Millie. This is Jill. But I'll get Millie. Hang on."

"No," I tried to say, "I want to talk to Kim." But I was too late. Jill was calling Millie.

John came on the line then. "Hello, this is Mr. Martin. My wife is busy at the moment, but I'd be glad to take a message. Say, this is a poor connection, isn't it? Who did you say was calling?"

"John, it's Al," I said louder. But just then I heard more interference. The extension had been picked up and Jill's puffing and panting came over the line.

"Millie was upstairs [huff, huff] but she's here now; hang on again. . . ." Faintly I could hear Jill instructing Millie to speak up.

"*Hello?*" Millie shrieked in her high voice.

This surprised John, who still didn't know who was calling his wife. He immediately directed his conversation at her. "Oh, I'm sorry, dear, I just told this caller you were away from the phone. I'll get off the line, then. This is really a bad hookup; be sure to talk loudly."

I was working on a headache. "Millie," I said slowly and clearly. "This is Al. Al Palmquist."

"Oh, Al!" she exulted joyfully. "It's you! Oh, I wish you were here. The most exciting thing . . . but you shouldn't be talking to me. Kim will want to tell you herself. Now you just hold the line and let me put Kim on. Can you wait there a minute?"

"Sure," I bawled. There was every danger of waking Julie and Ricky. Gayle went to close their door.

Forgetting to hang up the extension, Millie called out loudly and finally Kim picked up the downstairs phone.

"Hi, Al."

"Kim? Can you talk any louder?"

"O.K.," she answered. "Al, hang on a second . . . Jill, ask Millie if she put the phone back upstairs, would you?" I heard a scraping sound and then a click.

"Kim, Gayle said you called about something," I hollered.

"Yeah. Well, I . . . well, we . . . ah . . . oh, I don't know how to tell you. Let me think a minute . . . um . . . well, see, we all went to church tonight. At the Jesus People church. Do you know where that is?"

"Yes. Speak up, Kim."

"O.K., I'm trying. Well, anyway, the preacher talked about knowing Jesus the way you told me in the car the other day, remember?"

"Yeah." I swallowed, anticipation rising in my soul.

"And it all made sense but I had some questions about this 'Christian thing.' So when the service was over, John found this second-string preacher, like. A youth pastor or something. And he took me in his office and showed me from the Bible about Jesus' death and everything. He said it didn't matter what sins I had committed, that even if I were the only one in the world who had ever sinned, Jesus would have died just for me. Is that part true, Al?"

"Absolutely, Kim."

"What?"

This was the first time I had ever yelled about spiritual matters. "Absolutely, Kim," I repeated at five decibels.

"Well, then he said that being a Christian didn't mean going to church or becoming a missionary in Africa or giving away all your money or lighting candles or being 'holy'—it was just putting your trust in Jesus and what He did for you. I mean, for me. Like you said in the car. So, I . . . I prayed. He prayed first so I would know what to say. I didn't want to mess up in front of God!"

Apparently, everyone at that end had been eavesdropping, for I heard a happy uproar at this point and Kim must have dropped the phone. No matter, my ear was already ringing. And now my eyes were running. "Thank You, Lord," I breathed. "Thank You, thank You, thank You!"

Kim finally recovered the receiver and I welcomed her into God's family, telling her how pleased I was. "If you study the Bible now, Kim, you will find out what it means to be a child of God."

"I know, I know," she shouted. "John already told me I'd have to start memorizing Scripture verses. Yuk, I hate memorizing. But he said it would help me. I hafta go, Al," she yelled. "Connie is scarfing all the pizza."

"Thanks for telling me, Kim."

Wiping my face on my sleeve, I hung up and turned to Gayle. "Guess what?" I yelled, forgetting to lower my voice. "Kim got saved tonight!"

"I think everyone in south Minneapolis heard it, Al," Gayle smiled wryly. "But Jenny thought you were scolding her, honey. She's under the kitchen table pouting."

»10«

Recruiting

Nothing about Kimberly Pringle was ordinary.

After contacting the four girls I had arrested at Billy the Pimp's "stable"—two of whom agreed to testify against him if Kim would, which, I assured them, she certainly would—I went out to see her.

"No!" she responded.

"Kim, you must not understand," I replied patiently. "You see, two of the other prostitutes will testify against Billy if you will. I know it will be hard, but you won't be alone. We'll see that you are protected, we'll be there in the courtroom with you and, above all, Billy will be put in prison. For years and years if we win, which is almost certain with three testimonies. You will have a topnotch attorney, too. He'll help."

"No," she repeated with a shake of her head.

"Kim," I said, not quite as patiently. "You're not being reasonable."

"I can't! I just can't."

"Kim," I said, not patiently at all, "please don't start that again! I thought you were over your fear of Billy. You seemed to have no trouble talking about him when you learned he was in jail."

"But I can't look at him. I can't see him."

Like I said, nothing about her was ordinary. "Why can't you look at him?" I sighed, leaned back, and closed my eyes.

She fidgeted. "Because."

"Because why?"

"Because . . . his eyes scare me. Billy . . . Billy can control girls with his eyes."

I looked up. She was genuinely frightened. I went over and sat on the arm of the sofa she had adopted and gave her a hug. "All right, I'm listening now. I really am, Kim. Tell me about Billy's eyes."

Kim took a deep breath and began. "When a pimp recruits a girl he spends a lot of time working on her head, brainwashing her, like." She stopped. "Do you know how girls are recruited?"

"I don't know much," I said, moving to a comfortable chair nearby. "I heard that girls hooked on drugs will work for a pimp who'll supply them."

She grinned. "You're right."

"That's how girls are recruited?"

"No . . . you don't know much!"

I threw a pillow at her.

Kim continued. "Well, actually, that part is true but most girls, and I mean most, are not on drugs when they become prostitutes. Sure, they may have tried pot or something, but they're not really hooked." She interrupted herself. "Remember, Al, I only know about street pimps. There are different categories: sauna owners, corporation pimps, and the real big-timers, but I couldn't tell you nothin' about them.

"Well, anyway," she continued, "what street pimps try to do is find runaways. All the other girls in Billy's stable were runaways; two from South Dakota, one from Iowa, and the other from a small town in southern Minnesota. They had each hopped a bus to 'the big city' and Billy found them right at the bus station. 'Like pickin' peaches,' he said once.

"I went with him a few times and even I could tell the difference between the girls who happened to be traveling alone and the real runaways. Runaways look sorta depressed. They're scared and nervous, usually. The prostitutes I talked to, almost all of 'em, told me they were always having hassles at home so one day they got fed up and just took off.

"There was this one hustle, I think you could say it was typical, O.K.? The bus pulled in and this green chick got off—I mean, she was *so* dumb. She just stood around for a few minutes, watching everything. You could tell she didn't know what to do. Billy snapped his fingers real cocky-like and said, 'Watch this.' Then he went over to her and smiled and said, 'Wow, baby, has anyone ever told you that you are one fine looking lady?' The girl blushed and Billy said, 'Hey, I bet you need bread, right? How would you like to make at least two hundred dollars a day?' He acted so cute and friendly she finally laughed and nodded her head. Billy picked up her bag then and said, 'Well, let's talk about it. How 'bout some dinner? You hungry? Oh, by the way, honey, my name is Billy DuMont and I'm with the Better Girl Modeling Agency. I been lookin' all week for someone like you. You're the perfect size. Your hair and eyes are great and, well, honey, I hope you don't get the wrong idea, but your body is just right for this job.'

"The poor kid was in his hip pocket by this time. I went back to his place for the heavy stuff later. I don't know what he said to her over dinner, but it was probably the same line he used on us—like, he knew she was just breaking out on her own and maybe she needed a place to stay; would she like to stay in his building, it was sort of a commune with other people around so she wouldn't have to worry about anything funny going on, and so on. When they got back to the apartment she was spaced out already so Billy probably put something in her drink; he did that a lot.

"So anyway, it was almost two hours later when they walked in. We were doing weed—five or six other hookers, three of Billy's pimp friends, and me. Billy introduced her as a new friend named Mary, and he offered her some pot. She said she had smoked before but I didn't believe it. I mean, she didn't know what to do! And our pot was laced with coke. . . ."

"Cocaine?"

"Yeah, cocaine, so it wasn't ten minutes before she was stoned. She fell right off the big pillow she was sitting on."

Kim stopped talking and stared into space awhile.

"What? What's the matter?"

After a minute she said, "It gets pretty rough at this point, that's all. I don't like thinking about it."

"Look, Kim, if this hurts you, don't. . . ."

She turned to face me, her face cold and her jaw set. "If I don't tell you the rest you'll never understand about Billy's eyes." She looked away and added, "You probably won't anyway. No one does unless they've been there."

After a painful break, Kim finished, speaking quickly. "Mary was taken to the bedroom where she was stripped and all the pimps took turns raping her. It took a long time, maybe an hour, and everything was put on videotape. When a pimp finished with Mary, he put lots of money in her hand or on the nightstand. This happened over and over."

"Was Mary unconscious?" I asked.

"No. She probably thought she was having a dream. She was aware of what was happening but was too far gone to care.

"When the pimps were done, they let Mary sleep it off. But when she woke up they made her watch the tapes. It was horrible. Mary screamed and screamed but they forced her to watch every single thing. Then they started it over. She tried to run at first, but I was closest to the door and stopped her. Then she tried putting her face between her legs but the pimps held her.

"This was all part of the brainwashing. They wanted her to see herself as a hooker, a whore. They wanted her to know she was no longer a virgin; she belonged to the men. She was a woman who took money for sex.

"But that wasn't all of it. By this time, Mary was depressed, ashamed, humiliated, and sorry she'd ever left home. But a pimp needs to control his stable, even when he's not around. So he uses pain.

"After the tape was played two or three times, Billy came to Mary and held her close, telling her he was her 'main man,' her 'Big Daddy.' He said he would be real good to her but first she had to take care of some of his friends. Naturally, every man on the street is a friend of Billy's 'cause they make him rich.

"Well, Mary made a break for it and Billy dragged her back, telling her that really made him mad and he would have to teach her a lesson. He grabbed a thin wire hanger out of the closet, straightened it out, and made the end into a little hook. And he beat her. That's where the little horseshoe marks come from. Mary kept trying to get away but Billy was too strong for her. He beat her until she stopped resisting. All she wanted to do was die. She had screamed herself hoarse and there was blood all over the floor.

"He told one of the girls to run the bathtub full of warm water; then he helped Mary get over to the bathroom. He was real calm and nice by now. Then he dumped a bag of salt into the water and made Mary get in. She was so weak. And the water hurt so bad. She sobbed and screamed and promised Billy she would do whatever he wanted, anything, if he would only let her get out of the tub.

"Billy decided when she had had enough. He let her get up, dried her off, and took her to the bedroom. I think he raped her again, too, and probably told her she was really special to him and he didn't ever want to do that to her again, that he loved her and cared for her and just wanted her to stay with him always."

"Why do you think he said that to Mary?" I asked. It was impossible to believe all this. Kim sounded sincere but she must have fantasized part of it.

"Because that's what he said to me," she answered quietly. "And I believed him, not because he was telling the truth but because I wanted to believe him."

"Kim. . . ."

"I told you," she said. "I told you you probably wouldn't understand. But it's true. Every word of it. Some girls may not need the beating, not at first, anyway. And other kinds of pain may be used. Electric shocks, maybe. Or a fist. Did you see all the rings on Billy's hand? I saw him crack a girl's skull with those rings."

"How were you recruited?"

"Same way," she replied, then laid her head down on the pillow I'd thrown at her earlier. She looked drained. "Dad came home drunk and started yelling about the house. I yelled back at him. The house *was* a mess but it was all his beer cans and booze bottles and cigarette butts and under-wear. He made me so mad! So I slammed the door and ran. I'd been thinking about it, anyhow, and a girl from my school kept saying she knew all these black dudes who hung around the I.D.S. Building downtown. I decided to check it out."

"Is that where you met Billy?"

"Uh huh. He said I was foxy and invited me to have a joint at his place. Everything else was like Mary's story except I didn't fight so hard to get away, so he didn't beat me as long."

Kim shuddered. "I don't want to look at Billy, Al. I feel . . . his eyes make me feel like a robot or a puppet or a dog, maybe. Like I'm in his power and I'm helpless."

And then she began to cry.

»11«

It's All True

I was not convinced. Kimberly believed the story she had told me, of that I had no doubt. But it was too bizarre, too outrageous; she was believing a fantasy. The pimps, for instance: She had lifted them out of history, from Nazi Germany in the days of Hitler when twisted, perverted men took pleasure in watching people suffer. There was a flaw in her story, too: the drugs. Drugs were sold to customers; she had already told me that. They were not handed out like candy: dropped in drinks, given to friends, supplied endlessly to the "working girls," as Kim had said. A girl hooked on drugs would be no good to a pimp. Eventually she wouldn't be able to work.

But the biggest reason I could not believe Kim was that, according to her, any girl on the street could be turned into a whore in less than twenty-four hours. No way, José, I thought.

Still, I seemed to spend more time patrolling the bus station and the I.D.S. Building. There were a lot of "dudes" hanging idly around but I never saw any real action.

One evening toward the end of July I settled my tired body in front of "Police Story," a television series based on factual accounts from Los Angeles police files that I tried not to miss. This show was a rerun, but I'd missed the first showing.

In the opening scenes a runaway girl who had taken a bus

to Los Angeles was met, inside the station, by a twenty-year-old black man dressed in the typical flashy costume. He was warm, charming, and kind, and told the girl how beautiful she was. Then he offered to show her a way to make some big money—two or three hundred dollars a day, he said—by working for him. The work would be easy.

Well, she asked, what kind of work did he have in mind?

Oh, just a little modeling was all. Would she like to talk about it over dinner?

The scene switched to his apartment where ten or twelve young people were having a party. Shortly the man and the runaway came in. The booze, pot, and pills were plentiful and when the girl was offered some, she agreed to try a little, not wanting to seem square.

I sat up. Go ahead, tell us the pot is laced with cocaine, I thought.

Then the camera zoomed in to reveal the pot being laced with cocaine.

I could have narrated the story after that . . . the runaway became stoned, the guys gang raped her (this was not shown, of course, but the inference was unmistakable), and all the rapes were filmed. Next morning there was the crying, the beating, the screaming, the brainwashing, and the runaway was forced to sell herself. When she tried to run away time after time, she was considered too much trouble and was killed. Then the show ended.

That little brat, I thought angrily. Kim saw the first showing and merely put herself and "Mary" into the story. That explained it.

But I was more angry with the show. The writer was a policeman and had, I felt, allowed the Hollywood producers to "spice" things up to make the show sell. I felt ripped off; "Police Story" had lost every shred of its credibility for me.

There was no point in yelling at Kim, though I intended to mention it after I cooled off. What I did do was sit down and start a scorching letter to the network and the L.A. police force. Someone with police experience had to protest. They had no right to con the public like that!

The next day I left for work early so I could run up and talk to the Vice cops. "Hey, did you guys see 'Police Story' last night?" I asked. It was a favorite with the cops I knew and most of these men had seen it.

"And the first one last winter, too!" one joked.

"I got steamed," I said. "But just for the record, does that kind of thing ever happen? Was any of it true?"

Most of the men snickered. "Well, no, not entirely," one of the older men answered. "You know the part where the pimps filmed themselves raping her? That wasn't explained very well. That tape is actually shown to the new whore over and over so she sees herself as a prostitute. They'd probably film money being laid beside her after they'd used her.

"How much do you want to know?" he continued. "They get kicks from some real masochistic rot. A pimp might carve on her flesh or bust her up with his fists or go for some animal sex. . . ."

I held up my hand for him to stop, then slumped into a chair. "But what about all the drugs?"

"You mean the dough? Use your head, Palmquist. That's peanuts compared to what a chick can get on the street for her man. Outside of rent and his pimpmobile it's about the only overhead a pimp has." He chuckled. "If he pays his rent."

"But a hooker hooked on drugs can't be any good for business," I said.

He shrugged. "Dime a dozen, baby; dime a dozen. By the time she's really washed up she's made him more money than you make in a year."

"What about the timing? They made it look like you can run out and pick up a girl, any girl, and twenty-four hours later you've got yourself a prostitute."

"Depends. They take as long as they need. I've seen 'em breaking in a green chick on the streets at three or four in the morning. If that's what it takes, they do it. But psychologically, the pimp's got her under control in twenty-four hours, yeah. It's the pain. It's nothing new, Palmquist. Pick up any history book and you can read the same thing. Pain is fast, effective, and foolproof. Through pain, a pimp can program a girl's mind to think he's watching her every second of every day... like Santa Claus! Remember when you used to think the old guy was watching you all the time?" He laughed.

"Next you'll tell me there's no Easter Bunny," I said.

"Hey, Preach!" I heard across the room. "C'mon over here. Got something to show you. You've been too sheltered down there in Juvenile."

Apparently I had, because in all my years as a cop I had never seen pictures like those I was shown that day. There were dozens of shots of murdered prostitutes, many in full color. The tame pictures showed beatings and gun shots. Other girls had been burned or slashed or axed or carved up. One had been set on fire after gasoline was poured over her body. Another had taken an acid bath.

These pictures were to end up in my files the day, years later, when I would read the Youth Survey results stating that girls had no pimps, that there was little violence associated with prostitution.

I was dangerously close to vomiting. Every girl was a teenager. And each of them had been Midwestern girls—girls from Iowa, the Dakotas, Wisconsin, rural Minnesota, as well as the Twin Cities. I couldn't blame this on some faraway, unenlightened culture.

It's true, it's true, it's all true, I told myself. I turned a corner that day. These were children we were talking about. They had been deceived, tricked into prostitution; they were not adults who had made the choice after weighing the risks and consequences. They were being lured away, led away, or stolen away from their homes by a new, vile brand of twentieth century Pied Piper.

That day I knew we would open our home for kids. I knew the Lord would help me find some people who would give all it took, whatever it took, to see that those kids were safe.

»12«

Abducted!

August moved into Minnesota, hot and humid. With new determination I lined up churches, community groups, service clubs, and business people—anyone who would lend an ear to our plea. A makeshift Board of Directors was called together to help, too. Slowly, the wheels were beginning to move.

Billy's trial date was coming up, two months after his arrest, and Kim finally had agreed to testify. John took her down to the courtroom one day, showing her exactly what to expect, and she felt more confident. "I can look at you guys if you *promise* to sit on that side of the room," she told John. John reached into his pocket for a scrap of paper on which he wrote, "Reserved for John Martin and friends"; then he tagged one of the "approved" rows with it. Kim nodded solemnly. She could handle it.

The week before the trial was blistering. Minneapolis was hosting a huge convention so parking spots were almost nonexistent, and I always was soaked after the long walk from my car to the police station. On Wednesday, dashing and dripping, I slid into my chair as roll call began.

"Did it ever occur to you to leave home earlier?" Pete whispered. He looked crisp and sharp. As usual. Then he further embarrassed me by holding his nose briefly.

"I hope you spill ice cream on yourself!" I shot back.

113

When I was finally cool and comfortable again, we were dismissed and it was time to go back out on the streets. Back to the heat. "I'm gonna check my mail first," I called to Pete. "You going to Harry's for dinner?"

"I kind of like your idea of ice cream," Pete called back. "Let's do that joint over on Tenth tonight. Seven o'clock all right? I had a big lunch."

"I'll call you if it isn't."

I had bought myself a big briefcase when I became wise to the fertile and reproductive powers of the mails. I don't know what other people use their briefcases for, but mine was a creative marvel. With any luck, I could toss things into the jumbled interior, snap the lock, carry it to the car, and the items would never be seen again. I even lost a gun like that once. Friends used to make me pledge not to put such-and-such into my briefcase because they wanted it back. Gayle says the same thing about washing machines: You put in a pair of socks and take out a single. It's a fact of life.

I hoisted said briefcase onto a desk in the now-vacant meeting room and flicked the day's cards, circulars, notices, memos, and messages one by one into the jumbled interior.

One tiny slip of paper bearing only two short words caught my eye and I snatched it up. "Kim's gone."

I stared dumbly, unable to comprehend. Then an icy grip tightened around my heart and I could hardly breathe.

"Al, she was only going to walk to the store to pick up some suntan lotion," Millie said when I arrived. Her face was contorted with fear. "It shouldn't have taken her twenty minutes. That was four hours ago. We can't find her and I'm so worried!" Millie was shaken.

"Come on, now," I soothed with more optimism than I felt. With the other girls gathered around, we tried an entire recital of "maybes," but the girls would not be consoled. They believed the worst. All Kim's clothes were still in her closet and a bathing suit had been tossed on the bed. Clearly, she had intended to get some sun.

I searched her room, looking for a note. I found none, but spotted something white beside her not-so-new Bible. Crossing to the nightstand, I leaned down and picked it up. Except for a few faint stains, it was a new handkerchief. The initials "AP" were monogrammed in the corner.

It was a moment before I could speak to the girls, and when I did, I'm afraid I was not much comfort to any of them. Persuaded that Kim really could be in danger, I ran for the car, stuffing the handkerchief into my pocket. "I'm gonna start looking and I'll call you every hour," I shouted over my shoulder. "Pray!"

I was sure she had not gone back to Dewey's house, but I checked anyway. Neighbors had not seen her, nor had several old school friends. Then I cruised Lake Street, a neon jungle of street life. I searched every alley and dark corner of Minneapolis that held even a slight hint of promise, but she was nowhere.

There was only one thing left to do. I had put it off for it meant admitting Kimberly had been abducted—Billy's trial was imminent. But time was running out and there was no choice. My head throbbed.

Hennepin Avenue is to Minneapolis what Eighth Avenue is to Midtown New York: The strip sleeps late but comes out at night, smiling, twinkling, flirting, dressed up, and brassy. I made several passes up and down Hennepin, which was wide awake and swinging by this time, but Kimberly was not to be found. So I nosed my vehicle—it was an unmarked car and I was not in uniform—into a parking spot where I could observe unseen. Pimps drove long, shiny pimpmobiles back and forth, riding herd on their girls who were out in full force working the street.

I hated it! I hated the corruption, the filth, the sin of it all;

I hated the market that created pimps and prostitutes, and I hated more the twisted selfishness that drove men to buy such defilement and abuse women and children so. Above all, I hated the wicked deception that fed on little girls, teenagers, our daughters and even our sons, violating their fragile lives, ripping them away from us, damaging them, scarring them, very often torturing and murdering them.

I waited and watched. These people from the community of whores, pushers, hookers, and pimps had the information I needed, I was certain. The only way to wrench that information from them was to hold something over their heads. My plan was to nab one of them for a criminal offense, then trade a jail term for a tip. It would work, too, for like all human beings, they were selfish. They had sold out to this corruption, and they would sell out to me if the offer were attractive enough.

A little man shuffled slowly down the sidewalk, gazing in wonder at the brightly-lit travesty. He was the picture of innocence and vulnerability. He was my bait! Quickly I slipped out of my car and crossed the street, feigning interest in a nearby movie bill as the vultures closed in on the poor fellow. Two attractive blonds greeted him as warmly as granddaughters, telling him how nice he looked, stroking his arm, smoothing his lapel, cooing over his beautiful white hair. Delighted with the attention, the unsuspecting gentleman chattered and smiled with pleasure.

The streetwalkers were not offering their bodies to him, however; they were setting him up. One was particularly outgoing, so while she kept the old man busy, the other deftly slipped his wallet from a hip pocket into her bag.

Time for action.

Flashing my badge, I ordered the girls to produce ID's. Neither could. Expecting them to make a run for it, especially since I was working alone, I used a trick Pete had shown me: I handcuffed the girls to each other. Even if they did run

116

they would waste precious time and effort pulling against each other deciding which way to go. I'd never yet lost a cuffed twosome.

My little man was the nervous type and, in the excitement, began a nonstop soliloquy, none of which made sense. He "oh-my'd" and "oh-me'd" and "oh-dear-dear-dear'd" until I took hold of his shoulder kindly. "Sir," I said, "have you any identification?"

"Well, oh, uh-huh, mmm, I see, well, dear me now, oh for goodness sake, well, I don't, it should, oh my, I can't seem to, oh dear me. . . ." The panic rose in his voice as he fumbled with his clothing and realized his wallet was missing. Under his white hair, his face paled to a nearly matching shade until I became concerned for his blood pressure.

The hookers were quiet, their eyes brazen. "What was in your wallet?" I asked the man while scrutinizing the girls angrily. I hoped they were miserable.

"Oh, it's gone, it's gone," he wailed. "Oh my, oh dear God, what will I tell . . . oh, Officer, there was money, lots of money in my wallet! I just cashed my Social Security, don't you know . . . and credit cards . . . and my house key. . . ." He was trembling.

"I think I know where it has gone," I advised him. Instantly he was upon me. "You do? You think you know? Oh, do you think . . . perhaps you saw me drop it? Oh, can you find it? Oh, Officer, sir, I would be so grateful to you. . . ."

The girls volunteered nothing. "Open it!" I ordered. How they could just stand there watching the poor old man in agony I could not fathom! The bearer of the incriminating evidence acted as if she hadn't heard, but I continued to glare until she slowly opened her purse, revealing a fine old worn wallet.

For the first time, the dear old man was speechless. I took the wallet, opened it, and asked, "Is your name Phillip James

117

Owen?" Philip James Owen merely stood, lips quivering, eyes fixed on the guilty party.

"Sir, is this your wallet?" I asked, grasping his shoulder again. As in a trance, the man's eyes traveled slowly from the hooker's face to his beloved wallet and he took it reverently, clutching it to his heart. Then he began to weep.

I took out a pen and scribbled Mr. Owen's name and address and asked him to confirm them. He grieved with remarkable dignity for another moment, then found his voice again. Yes, yes, that was certainly his current address, sir, and did I need his phone number? He blew his nose gustily, then heaped enormous gratitude upon me, declaring himself a foolish old soul and offering a reward for my kindness. He was a delight, and I was glad I'd been on hand to help him. I sent him straight home, where I am certain he went, chattering all the way.

The girls went straight to my car. I reached for my arrest reports, then said casually, "I need something from you."

"Oh, sure," they chorused eagerly, asking what kind of sex I liked, saying they would be happy to oblige me in any little ol' way they could. Anything I wanted they could provide, honey.

"And I'm willing to trade your arrest for it," I continued, ignoring their offers. "I want information. *Only* information."

They looked at each other and shrugged. "What kind of information?"

"I'm looking for a kid named Kimberly Pringle. Used to work for Billy DuMont before we locked him up." I told them she had been out of circulation awhile but probably came back tonight.

When I described her, one girl snapped her fingers. "I bet he means Kitten! Her old man's a pig...I mean, cop, isn't he? That's Kitten. Yeah, I saw Jake with her over on Fifth just a little while ago. She ain't back on the street, though, honey. Jake wasn't lettin' her out of the car. Even if he had, she couldn't have walked half a block . . . she was far away, baby. Far away."

"What do you know about Jake?" I struggled hard to stay calm.

"Let me tell you something, mister," the pickpocket said, leaning closer and narrowing her eyes. "I would go any-where—kill myself, even—before I'd work for that freak! Ain't nobody as mean as Jake. I'll tell you somethin' else, too, long as you're buyin'—word's out that Jake's movin' into the New York scene. If he's got your Kitten—Kimberly or what-ever her name is—you can kiss her goodbye, baby!" She leaned back. "It ain't pretty here," she said, looking out at the street, "but New York is the pits, man."

I felt faint. And I had to hurry. The pickpocket was able to supply Jake's license number, on which I ran a make. (A lot of prostitutes, I had learned, had a propensity for numbers.) Waiting for the results, I got a description of Jake. "And his apartment is on Golden Valley Road someplace," my tipster added.

The make came back and she was right. I thanked them for their help, suggested they find other employment, and prac-tically threw them out of the back seat in my haste. Tires screeching, I flew toward Golden Valley, overlooking any small infractions of the law I may have observed.

This time there was no pimpmobile in the driveway to test for engine heat. There were no voices floating down the hall, no creaky steps, and no one to surprise with my crashing entrance. The place was a mess. Food, clothes, tapes and records, dishes, beer cans, and wine bottles were all over the floor. The furniture was all there. But no clothes hung in the closets. I went into the bathroom . . . no toilet articles.

I was too late! Helplessly I wandered through the rooms, looking for a clue, anything that could help me. My foot caught on a long wire and I bent down to pick it up. So Billy's technique was not unique. Great shuddering sobs rose in my throat as I fingered the device and then I hurled it brutally against the wall. It was a wire coat hanger, opened and twisted into a long whip with a tiny hook at the end. The horseshoe hook was covered with dried blood.

»13«

BBSN-25

It was too early to file a Missing Persons report, but I phoned my Sergeant to ask that Dewey be notified of his daughter's abduction. And I phoned the Jesus House, grateful to talk to John who would break the news to Kim's other "family." Shortly I was back on Hennepin searching for a Continental, license plate number BBSN-25. There was almost no chance I would find it, but I had to do something.

What would I do if I found it, I wondered? Perhaps there would be some small violation I could use on Jake: bald tires, driving over the center line, failure to come to a complete stop, failure to signal, anything.

One time, when I was new on the force, my partner gave me a demonstration of how to take pimps out of circulation awhile. We were patrolling Lake Street when Mac, who was a rough character, spotted a pimpmobile. We followed it for a few miles, then Mac flipped on the red lights and pulled him over.

"What'd he do?" I asked in surprise.

"Just you watch."

I trailed along to the driver's side where Mac asked the pimp for his license. Handing it over, the pimp objected to the injustice. "Man, I ain't done nothin' wrong! Now, what'dja go and stop me for, anyhow? I done nothin' wrong, fuzz!"

Mac proceeded, "It is my duty to inform you that you are under arrest. Your tail light is out."

The pimp got really agitated. "Oh, man, I *knows* there's nothin' wrong with this here automobile!" But the pimp was wrong. As Mac approached the car, he had taken a jab at the tail light with the business end of his rugged five cell flashlight. The pimp was definitely wrong.

People are often surprised to learn that a traffic ticket is actually an arrest. And a policeman has three ways to go when he makes an arrest. One, he can warn the violator; two, probably the most common, he can write a traffic ticket; and three, he can arrest the violator on the spot, take him to jail, and order his car impounded.

Mac elected to do the latter. He knew the pimp would stay in jail only a few minutes, but by the time he would pay his fine and wade through all the paperwork for himself and his car, possibly three hours would be eaten up; three hours in which he could not recruit new girls or keep track of his old ones.

Mac had been wrong to break out the tail light. But I understood why he did it. If I caught up with a Continental, license plate number BBSN-25, tonight, I was not so sure but what I'd do the same.

In the course of my search, I saw a long, white car run a stoplight on a quiet stretch of Hennepin beyond downtown. I pulled him over by placing my portable red light, held in place by several small magnets, on the metal roof. I always thought it looked so neat to see TV cops stick their portable lights on the roof when they got into chases, but the first time I had to do it in real life, I found that the magnets would not hold after about forty-five miles an hour. Throughout that entire first chase my light banged and crashed against the side window. The guy I was after was in hysterics over it.

Tonight there was no chase and my light did not fly off. As

soon as the driver saw the red flashing behind him, he pulled to the curb so quickly that his car gave the appearance of pivoting in a perfect right angle. My mind was intent on Kim as I absently went through the motions required in a moving violation. I hardly noticed the driver as I requested his license and recited his offense. Automatically I ran the number; automatically I walked back to his car; automatically I explained what to do with his ticket—pay it or plead "not guilty."

Attention focused on everything around me—sidewalks, doorways, streets, and alleys—I handed his license back and wished him good night. He said nothing but left in a bit of a hurry, I felt. I returned to my car and felt around in the dark for the carbon copies of the tag. Gradually it all came back to me: I'd forgotten to write the ticket.

My face flushed with embarrassment and I might have laughed, had the circumstances been different. Instead I reached deep into my pocket to grasp hold of something clean and white; a handkerchief, some would call it. But it was more than that to me. Much more.

»14«

Midwest Challenge Is Born

"Gayle, did my blue pinstripe come back from the cleaners?" I asked breathlessly after sprinting up the walk, scaling the front steps in one leap and bursting into the house.

Gayle turned around in time to see two pantlegs and two worn shoes disappearing up the stairs. "Oh, hello, dear, and how was your day?" she asked in exaggerated fashion. "Well, just fine, thank you, sweetheart," she continued, "and how was your day? You know, it's nice to see you . . . I missed you too, darling; I simply could not wait to get home and come rushing into your arms, my pet . . . oh, you beast, you silly beast!"

"The woman's taken leave of her senses," I told Jenny. But the cunning reproach had worked and I hurried back to the kitchen. "I'm sorry," I said, nuzzling her neck and sneaking a hunk of the melon she was slicing. Then I turned her face for a long kiss and asked tenderly, "Now . . . is my suit back?"

"Oh, Al!" she scolded. "I don't know. Check the closet. Why?"

"Church meeting, and I'm late," I yelled on my way upstairs again. "I don't have time to eat. Save me some, huh?"

Showered, shaved, and freshly dressed, I stuck my head

into the kitchen where my family sat quietly having dinner. Then I felt guilty. I looked at Gayle. "What's the matter?"

"I'm pouting, I suppose," she said. "I forgot about your meeting and I asked Mom to babysit. There's a new shopping center open and I thought it would be fun to go look around. Maybe stop for coffee after. How come you're so late, anyway?"

"I've been house hunting all afternoon, Gayle," I said irritably. "It's not like I was out shooting pool, you know. I'm dog-tired and this is an important meeting tonight. I don't see how you could have forgotten it!"

"Well, you've got your precious suit, haven't you? Why are you yelling at me?"

"I thought you were in this thing with me!" Throughout the "discussion" we monitored our voices so Julie and Ricky would not notice that a quarrel was brewing. As if they had no eyes or ears or feelings.

"That's not fair," Gayle objected heatedly.

She was right; it wasn't fair. But I was angry and I was in a hurry. "Gayle, I have to go. Here's ten dollars—why don't you borrow Mom's car and just get out of the house awhile? I'll see you when I get home."

Why did I do that? I asked myself in the car. I had known immediately it was the wrong thing to say—I would resent Gayle trying to buy me off like that. Why was I so hotheaded, anyway?

I took a long, deep breath and tried to relax. It was everything. It was Kim's disappearance three months ago and hearing no word from her. It was the Project. (I'd begun thinking of it as having a capital "P" since we referred to it so often.) Though the response was picking up we still had so far to go. And my commitment to the Project only complicated things, for now we could no longer "try" it. We could not fail. It must be done.

And it was this meeting tonight. Pastor Gordon Peterson

had invited me to take part in a big service at his downtown church, Soul's Harbor. The featured speaker was Nicky Cruz, a gang leader from the ghetto who had met Jesus through Teen Challenge and was now a popular youth speaker. Nicky was an old friend and I was looking forward to seeing him; I also wanted to do a good job tonight and I felt a little tense.

Besides everything else, I was tired.

We had a good crowd and Nicky was terrific. His message, given in a voice still thick with a Puerto Rican accent, was earnest and moving and many young people walked forward at the end to ask Jesus to be their Savior.

Standing in the back afterward, I was answering questions and chatting with friends when I saw a tattered young man make his way through the crowd. He told me, in a shaky voice, that he was a drug addict who needed help kicking his habit. Then he began unfolding his life, explaining how he'd gotten mixed up in drugs.

I was amazed. "Doesn't it bother you to tell a police officer that you are hooked on drugs?" I asked.

"Oh, man, so what?" he replied. "I dig that program you're gonna start. So you're a cop? It don't matter, man. Once the word gets around that you're straight and you ain't out to rip us off, we'll trust you. We know we can't con a cop, see? If you play it cool, don't use us, or land us in the slam, you'll have more of us dopers than you can handle."

He talked more of his deep desire to kick his habit, then slipped back into the crowd. Before disappearing, though, he called, "Hey, man, hurry and open that center. I'll know when it happens and you better believe I'll be there."

It never failed, I thought, shaking my head. Each time I was headed for rock bottom, God sent something or someone along to yank me up and put me back on track. Hey, you addict, I said silently, one day we'll have a place for you, you hear? I'll just keep looking. We'll find one!

Going home, I drove along the river with my windows

down. Though winter was nearly here, enough of fall lingered in the air to catch one last whiff. The weather had been great all week and it felt good to relax and enjoy it. If Gayle were here, I'd reach for her hand or put my arm around her to share the experience. Suddenly I ached for her companionship.

I hurried, then. When I opened the door of the quiet, dimly lit house, I saw the ten-dollar bill exactly where I had put it, on the kitchen table. Gayle looked up from her book.

"I'm not in a hurry anymore," I ventured.

She smiled but said nothing.

"I'm mad at me for giving you money," I said.

"Good," she said. "Should've been at least twice that much."

I walked over to her and drew her close. "I'm sorry," we said at the same time. And we hugged and kissed and were sorry and declared that we loved each other. This went on for some minutes.

"Hey," I said, inspired. "Get your coat; there's something I want to show you."

"The kids . . ." she began.

"I'll ask Mrs. Inger to look in on them. We won't be long."

This done, we ran to the car and I drove to an address a few miles away. The house was big, three stories high and very run-down. "I had just come from here when I got home and started acting stupid," I told Gayle.

"I can see why," she responded, looking it over. "It's depressing."

"Now, yes. But I think it has possibilities."

"For the Project?"

"Yeah. What do you think?"

"I think it needs a lot of work before it's ready to be condemned."

"Well, you're wrong about that. It's just been condemned."

Gayle laughed. "Are you serious?"

"This is a recently condemned nursing home that is structurally built to last centuries. I wish I could show you the inside. It's a disaster but there is enough room to house a dozen kids, I'd guess. And they'll take twenty-four thousand for it, including furniture. Now look at it again and think 'twenty-four thousand, twenty-four thousand. . . .' It looks better and better, doesn't it?"

She laughed again. "Either you're really getting desperate, Al, or this is God's house for us. I guess we'll know which when it's time to pay the twenty-four thousand."

Since it was such a beautiful night, I decided to ignore such cold, hard financial considerations and, instead, drove slowly along the river. Gayle snuggled near and we shared the moonlight and the fragrance of autumn and the quiet water, just as I intended. Back home, we shared a cup of hot chocolate.

"Know what, honey?" Gayle asked dreamily, tucked into my arms.

"What?"

"I really do need twenty dollars."

Early in 1972 I was ready to present the house to our Board. Winter had passed, more church boards had put us in their budgets, I had looked for other houses but found no better values for the money, and some zoning problems had been worked out.

"The nursing home is on the market for twenty-four thousand dollars," I summarized, "and I think we should move on it."

One member asked how much money we had collected.

"Do you mean what has been promised, or what is in the checkbook?"

They wanted the checkbook amount. The actual cash.

"Sixty-four dollars," I replied.

We had a wonderful Board. Two minutes after the laughter

died down they voted to go ahead. But the weeks ahead were frantic. Now that we had a potential home we wanted a real name: Midwest Challenge, we decided. At the time, our thoughts were centered on Minneapolis drug addicts, so the "Midwest" part was a monument to our faith!

With a real home (still potential) and a real name, we began to attract real money from those who had promised to stand behind us. The countdown continued. Two weeks before the entire sum was due, we had several thousand dollars in the checkbook. A nice, round figure but not nearly enough.

The Board prayed. Gayle and I prayed. John and Millie and the girls prayed. Other friends prayed. And God answered. In His wisdom He made us wait until the very last morning, but every dollar came in.

I stood outside the front door of that shabby, dilapidated, pitiful house, holding the key in my hand, and cried. Hello there, Midwest Challenge, I said to the house. We've waited a long time for you! Had there been any way to hug a building, I'd have done so.

Only one thing would have made the moment sweeter. My thoughts carried me back nearly seven months. "Oh, God," I prayed. "You worked a miracle here. Miracles are nothing to you . . . could you please send Kimberly back to us, Father?"

The moment of victory past, we turned to the work. At first we busied ourselves carting out the trash and surveying the property, but soon the Health Department arrived for its inspection. The Inspector "hmmmm'd" mysteriously at each corner and produced little marks on his form. The source of his darkest "hmmmms" seemed to be lurking in the kitchen. Soon we heard his verdict: Remove the floor, remove the ceiling, remove the walls, and remove everything in between. Loosely translated.

"Oh, well, is that all?" someone commented. Actually, the

work was the least of our concerns; our toughest problem was, as predicted, finances. We had spent every cent buying the place.

I phoned the Mayor to ask if he could provide help for us—policemen who had been carpenters or handymen.

"Sure," Mayor Stenvig replied. "Tomorrow you'll have some muscle there at eight o'clock. How's that? By the way, congratulations, Al!"

Dressing for work the next day was a nice change from the norm. I left my suit hanging in the closet and pulled on my oldest jeans and a worn shirt. Then I drove to the new Midwest Challenge where I met the other officers, yesterday the image of authority but today a motley assortment of laborers. I repeated what I had been told, including the line from the Health Inspector about the kitchen. They all groaned but rolled up their shirt sleeves and dug in. The racket was deafening.

Later that morning during a lull, we heard a faint knock at the front door.

"Come in," we yelled in unison.

The door opened slowly and a very thin drug addict, slumped over and looking ill, advanced a few steps. He needed a shot of dope, I surmised. While the "carpenters" studied him, he asked, "This is Midwest Challenge, isn't it?"

"Yes," I answered with a smile. The surroundings did not look exactly like a place that could change lives, unless he was interested in becoming a wrecker.

"Gee, I'm glad to be here," he exclaimed in great relief as he sank weakly against the wall. "I've been running from the cops for weeks."

I heard a general rustling behind me as the carpenters learned this news. "What," I asked guardedly, "are you wanted for?"

"Parole violation, two counts of burglary, and auto theft."

"I see," I said, grabbing his arm quickly. "You'd better come on into my office." I thought it wise to get him away from the "crew," each of whom was working with a hammer, mallet, or crowbar. We definitely needed an atmosphere more suited to mutual trust.

My office was an enclosed end of the winterized front porch, just to the right of the front door. The area was sunny, handy, and adequately furnished, I felt, with an ironing board desk, a sawhorse chair, and a telephone. My guest sat; I leaned.

"The first thing I had better tell you," I began, "is that we are all police officers."

The junkie sprang from his sawhorse. "But there was this minister who said I could trust you guys at Midwest Challenge," he whimpered miserably. His eyes began darting in every direction, his entire manner like that of a moth trapped in a jar. Thoroughly fascinated, I had the strongest urge to hurl a net over him.

"Now hold on," I said at last, easing him back onto his sawhorse. "Not only can you trust me, I am going to phone the Chief of Police and ask for his help. How's that? You can't get much higher than that!"

The skinny junkie did not share my excitement, but, I reasoned, he's in a tight spot here. No wonder he's nervous.

The Chief was in and I proudly told him of our very first contact. "But I'm not sure what to do at this point, Gordy. What do you advise?"

"What is your new student's name?" Chief Johnson asked after expressing his enthusiasm.

"What's your name?" I asked, covering the mouthpiece.

The junkie squirmed uncomfortably. "Phil Evans," he whispered, gnawing at his bottom lip.

"Phil Evans," I whispered into the phone. Why were we whispering? "Phil Evans," I repeated in full voice, shaking my head. This kid was a basket case.

"What?" the phone thundered back. I jumped. Phil Evans jumped too. He almost melted over the sawhorse.

"What's the matter? What's the matter?" I yelled back at the Chief, looking at Phil Evans as though he was harboring a bomb. This entire matter was getting somewhat difficult.

I was told, in deafening tones, what troubled the Chief about Mr. Evans' name. It seemed that Phil Evans had taken a shot at Chief Johnson and his partner a few years earlier.

Gordy calmed down by degrees as he recalled the incident for me. I added a reminder that he must learn to forgive people, and Phil Evans nodded humbly in agreement.

Finally the Chief stopped steaming and asked for my phone number. "I'll call you when I've figured out what to do with him," he said.

I hung up. "Why didn't you tell me you had taken a shot at the Chief?" I demanded.

Wringing his hands, Phil answered, "Well, you didn't actually ask. . . ." His voice faltered and failed.

In minutes the Chief phoned back. "I've had Phil Evans put on special parole," he announced. "But give him this message from me: Tell him he had better behave himself or I will take care of him personally!"

I gave Phil the message.

"What does he mean, 'take care of him personally'?" Phil cried.

"I'm not sure," I said reverently. "The Chief has been a cop for many years. He often tells us how the detectives used to get a confession from a tight-lipped suspect by taking him down to the Third Avenue bridge and holding him by the heels over the Mississippi River.

"Once in awhile someone's shoes would fall off," I said ominously. "You'd better tie your shoes real tight."

Phil's eyes were huge. But when I grinned he relaxed and pried his fingers free of the wood.

Obviously, Phil couldn't stay with us yet. He was in need

of medical attention, so I signed him into the hospital for a few days, long enough for him to go through withdrawal and get some strength back.

Midwest Challenge, drug rehabilitation program, had begun.

»15«

A New Challenge

It was 3:00 A.M. and all the same to New York City. Some cities have twenty-four-hour grocery stores, laundries, and service stations. . . . New York City has twenty-four-hour filth. Strip joints, porno shops, peep shows, adult book stores (featuring every kind of full-color specialty sex magazine available), triple-X-rated movie houses, homosexual clubs, saunas and massage parlors, orgy marts, bars, drug dealers' hangouts, S/M (sadomasochism) galleries, and prostitutes. Always the prostitutes.

"Kitty" knew the score. Hard-hitting businessmen came into the city early and worked late. Maybe their wives hassled them; maybe their wives didn't care; maybe there were no wives. "I've had a rough day . . . believe I'll have a drink and maybe a little sex before I head home," they think. They select hookers as deliberately as they select whiskey sours. They finish with each in about the same amount of time, too, and set them aside to be forgotten. Or there were the good-time men, in town for their conventions, always ready for a party. Or there were adolescents, looking for experience before tackling the "real thing." Or there were misfits, feeling too shy or ugly to get girls to like them. Or there were the evil, depraved obsessives, with a glint of insanity in their eyes.

Kitty could handle them all. She had turned fourteen, and

135

*sometimes she could finish by 3:00 A.M. Not tonight, though.
She hadn't made her "nut" yet.*

*She laughed when she thought of her school friends.
Babies! she snickered. Going to school, to the movies, out
shopping, out on dates . . . they're sleeping right now, she
sneered. Dreaming pretty little dreams. Ha! What did they
know about this rotten, stinking life? What did they really
know?*

*Kitty picked her way around a wino sleeping under a scrap
of carpet and returned to her strip. Maybe just one more
score tonight, then she'd be able to sleep. It was misting a
little. Kitty wiped the moisture from her face. It didn't
matter—it was only a mask.*

A week after our initial acquaintance, Phil Evans brought
us our second and third students, too. He didn't intend to,
necessarily, but that was what happened.

I was doing inside duty again, a normal eight to five shift.
Checking over some files, I got the bright idea of looking up
Phil's record. My day had gone well until then. I should have
known enough to leave the file untouched when I first
spotted the "Evans" name: It was jammed with documents. I
counted fifty-four arrests. I had never seen a file so full.

"Pete," I called, "I have to see a guy about a dog—scratch
that; I have to see the dog, period. No, scratch that; I have
too much respect for dogs! I'll be back!"

Three miles and about three minutes later, I flew up the
Midwest Challenge steps. *"Evans,"* I screeched. Instantly,
Phil's brief body began to fade into the woodwork. He had
been released from the hospital a few days earlier and was
helping the "carpenters" put his new home in shape.

I might have missed the chameleonlike figure if the men
had not turned to stare at him. "Evans," I repeated, "why
didn't you tell me you had fifty-four arrests on your record?"

Phil's eyes began their little dance again, fluttering and

darting madly. His skinny arms patted his sides as he cowered in front of me, and his voice was stringy, like those on the old Victrolas. "Palmquist . . . I am sorry. But you . . . you . . . never asked me how many times . . . if I had been . . . about my arrests. I thought you would ask."

This sent my colleagues into fits of laughter and I paced around in angry humiliation. He was right—what kind of cop would forget to ask for an arrest record?

Still, something should be done. I couldn't figure out a fitting corrective measure. He was too old to stand in the corner.

"Come with me," I instructed. "You'll have to . . . ride with me awhile." At the moment it escapes me why I thought that would do any good, but I *had* taken action.

We had ridden in silence for only a few minutes when Phil spoke up. "Look, Al, there are two of my friends on that bus bench." I looked, quickly recognizing their sleepy, head-bobbing traits . . . they were strung out on heroin. Under a good deal of pressure from Phil, the two ended up in my squad car, on their way to Midwest Challenge as Students Two and Three. Giving no thought to the fact that his friends had broken parole by getting high and planning to flee Minneapolis, or to my duty as a sworn officer of the law, Phil told them enthusiastically that I had connections. "My friend, Al, knows the Chief of Police," Phil said. "He'll get you off!"

"Al, whatever happened to Kim's pimp . . . Billy, wasn't it?" John had surprised me with a visit to "The Project" house; he had not quite adopted the Midwest Challenge name yet.

"Well," I said, thankful for an excuse to put down my hammer and drink a glass of water, "when the two girls learned that Kim was gone, probably abducted, I think they got scared. They realized how much rougher a pimp could be on them. So they agreed to testify even without Kim there, and they won. Billy was sent to prison. The sentence was ten years, but I think he's eligible for parole in five. I don't remember for sure."

We were sitting in my office, which now had two genuine chairs and a somewhat wobbly desk. Just then the phone rang. While I talked to the caller, John reached over and picked up my police transcriber. Toying with it, he flipped the "on" switch and a familiar voice was heard.

"God, I have never prayed before but I think You're around here. I'd like to know more about You, God, if You could work it out. Could You help Al, too, God, with the big job he has to do? Oh, yeah, thanks for this food. Amen."

Watching John's shocked face, I had trouble concentrating on my caller. John rewound the tape and played it again, just to be sure. The third time he played it, tears flowed down his cheeks.

I hung up and found myself unaccountably embarrassed, as if caught in some mischief. I could think of nothing to say.

John drew out his handkerchief and wiped his eyes. When he finally spoke, his voice was gusty with emotion. "I must share this with Millie, Al. Please. It will be something for her to . . . hold."

I nodded. After a moment, I said, "Let me make you a copy. Your recorder won't take this size tape and, anyway, I still . . . need it."

John blew his nose then, and laid the transcriber tenderly on my desk. He gave it a tiny caress before withdrawing his hand. "I know, I know, Al. Millie and I have her picture and Bible on top of the piano." John struggled with the tears once more. "It's so hard, isn't it? So hard to wait."

From the beginning, Midwest Challenge was special. Chief Gordy Johnson and Mayor Stenvig both stuck their necks out to help us get started, not only because the social and political climate was right, but because they also understood our philosophy. They recognized that sin is at the bottom of the crime problem. When a lawbreaker faces his sin, places his trust in the death and resurrection of Jesus Christ, then submits himself to the biblical training and spiritual leadership of a local church, not only does a miraculous transformation take place in a human life, but the crime rate goes down as well.

When I was discouraged, they were there to buck me up. They never interfered, either, though they offered plenty of advice. They talked and they listened. They took a brave stand for the Midwest Challenge cause.

Brave, because Midwest was such a unique help program. In our first years we maintained a ninety-five percent cure ratio: that is, ninety-five percent of the kids who completed and graduated remained free of drug and alcohol use. Most became healthy members of community churches. In the ensuing years of Midwest's history, the cure rate would never drop below ninety percent.

Maybe that unique status was the program's problem, too. Midwest Challenge settled into the cracks where church and state divide. The legal, political, and governmental systems viewed Midwest as a highly successful rehabilitation effort and, as such, beneficial in the areas of crime prevention, crime reduction, and criminal rehabilitation. And all at no cost to the taxpayer.

The church, the source of most monetary support, saw Midwest as a "home mission," a ministry in which Jesus Christ was uplifted and which would not work outside the power of the gospel and the Word of God. To the church, the project was worthy of money and prayers; solid proof that the gospel changes lives. Midwest Challenge ministered to the church's own kids, their friends' kids, their community's kids.

For as long as Charlie Stenvig and Gordy Johnson were in office, Midwest Challenge was treated as a successful, viable alternative in criminal justice. When the courts sent us a young lawbreaker, we turned the Word of God and our professional counselors loose on him and, more than nine out of ten times, gave back to the community a repaired, productive citizen.

But ill winds began to brew. "There may not always be a sympathetic mayor in office," Stenvig warned me. He had felt the first breezes.

But I was so busy with *now* I hardly considered the future.

"You must hire the very best people to head up Midwest Challenge," Stenvig advised. "The idea is to work yourself out of a job."

Unthinkable, I said. These street kids and jailbirds and dopers and hookers are my friends. I like helping them. And I love police work. I would do both.

"Helping addicts is one thing," Stenvig and Johnson and others mused one day. "But you get to messing around in the prostitution industry and you'll have more trouble than you can handle. What you know about prostitutes and pimps is microscopic! Minneapolis has its share of street pimps— they're often black and they often come here from other cities to do their 'shopping.' But look at the massage parlors, the escort services, the corporation prostitution—look, but don't touch, Palmquist! A supply of friendly ladies there is as indispensable as the corporate water cooler. Those pimps are big guns—vice presidents, citizens in our own communities.

"Al, some of the Vice guys tell me that possibly seventy-five percent of the men in our country visit a prostitute at least once in their lifetime. You're in a tiny, tiny minority, pal! It will be one huge, uphill battle just to help a few teenaged streetwalkers. Are you willing to settle for that?"

I didn't know. But I wouldn't quit.

In time, I had four major career responsibilities: I was a full-time cop, the Executive Director for Midwest Challenge, the chief fund-raiser for Midwest, and a big part of the new police chaplaincy program. The latter involved training several dozen area ministers to work with the police in such duties as family fights and death calls. Again due to the efforts of Stenvig and Johnson, a number of cities throughout the United States adopted the design of the Minneapolis Police Chaplains Program.

Of the four, fund raising took the most time. Midwest Challenge began to be recognized as an established rehab center when graduating students went back home straight, clean, and stable. Soon I began receiving invitations to present our work. Eventually my calendar was filled. Night after night I drove to places further and further away to share what the Lord was doing.

"What makes Midwest Challenge different?" folks would ask. "Why does it work so well?" Compared to the low recovery rate of most government-funded programs, our over ninety percent rate looked amazing.

These questions were asked so often that, in true preacher style, I wrapped a sermon around the answer.

St. Augustine, I would begin, once stated that "Man is born with a God-shaped void." The Bible, too, declares that ". . . when we were enemies, we were reconciled to God by the death of his Son, much more, being reconciled, we shall be saved by his life" (Rom. 5:10 KJV).

Over and over, the Bible points out that man is hopeless, lost in sin, helpless to save himself from the punishment for sin. And man constantly looks for ways to fill the emptiness in his soul. Some may try to drown it in booze; others try to ignore it, turning instead to sexual perversions, drug abuse, and narcotics; some may deny the emptiness by becoming atheists or agnostics; some try filling the emptiness through counterfeit spiritual experiences; and some even try disregarding it by cramming their lives with work and activity.

A simple story, told in three of the four Gospels in the New Testament, illustrates that nothing can fill the emptiness but the God-man, Jesus Christ (see Matt. 19:16–26, Mark 10:17–27,

Luke 18:18–27). A man came to see Jesus, asking how to be born again so that he might have eternal life. He craved an answer, so he sought out the Teacher from Galilee. We're not told his name but he was referred to as the rich, young ruler.

He was rich. He could buy anything he wanted. Yet he was not satisfied. He was young, yet the youth for which so many strive did not blot out the unhappiness of this man. And he was a ruler. He had position and power. But he wanted more.

The rich, young ruler went away sorrowful, because he could not accept the answer Jesus gave: sell all he had—acknowledge his emptiness—and accept Jesus as God's Son.

I believe, and Midwest Challenge teaches, that the drug scene is one way people attempt to fill the emptiness within themselves. How? One, drugs can soften the pain of an unpleasant environment, producing a temporary, false peace. It may relieve the ache for a time. And two, the drug scene has been peddled oftentimes as *the way* to peace. The use of drugs becomes a substitute Savior in certain cults.

I picked up an interesting fact in the Old Testament when I began my study of drugs. The Bible does not distinguish between drugs and witchcraft. The use of drugs is, therefore, one version of satanic worship. This will not surprise us if we remember that Satan is a spiritual being who desires to be worshiped as god and that we humans, with our spiritual void, are driven to worship someone or something. One who takes drugs, then, releases the control of his mind; his mind is susceptible to Satan's power.*

But when one claims Jesus as Savior, sin is forgiven, the guilt and penalty of sin is removed, and a new life is provided. This is what Christ did for us when He died on the cross to pay our debt for sin (death) and rose from the grave

---

*This is not to say that everyone who takes drugs is under Satan's power, nor is everyone who does not take drugs free from his power. The mind is simply more susceptible to Satan when one is under the influence of an abused drug.

to make sin and death powerless over us. Any drug program that subscribes to these biblical concepts and truths will be a successful drug program! Jesus Christ and His powerful Word is our program. Midwest Challenge works because He works!

Very often, individuals from the groups and congregations I addressed would respond to this Good News, even those with no drug or alcohol problem. They realized their need of a Savior, no matter what their sin, and they simply told the Lord they needed *Him* because of what He did for them through His death and resurrection.

The Bible promises that Jesus Christ will become the Savior of any who place their trust in Him, I told these folks. That trust is also called faith.

I have found the thrill of leading someone to an understanding of the gospel, and then helping them respond in faith to that message, has never been equaled on this old earth!

»16«

Watching the Vision Grow

Kitty slowly opened her eyes to see the swirling, dancing colors. They were so graceful, so beautiful! They moved toward the sun, with its hot white light, and made music. Lovely, gentle music. Kitty embraced the music. It wrapped her in tender wisps, softly brushing her skin with silver flecks. Now it snowed the flecks, down, down, down, until they became a swelling, surging river.

She didn't like the river. Too strong. So she spread herself on the magic carpet and floated away. Away to the pretty reds and pretty blues and happy, tinkling leaves. Away to the warm, delicious clouds. Away . . . away.

"Get up!" Jake shouted. "Get up or I'll see that you never get up again! You took too much stuff," he screamed, kicking her brutally, "and you ain't gonna be no good to me, you _____! Now you get yourself out there and you bring back a wad, baby! You hear me, a wad! This ain't no free ride, baby. You gonna work for Jake!"

Kitty smiled slowly and tried to stand. If she could just hang on to something—there, that was it. Weaving, swaying, Kitty supported herself by leaning on the beautiful, chestnut mare. Tomorrow it would be a trash can again. Tomorrow.

The years since 1972, when Midwest Challenge began, deserve their own book. From my dream of opening one

145

home for Minneapolis drug addicts, we advanced in three years to owning seven houses. Each deserves a chapter in that book. But there are similarities in their histories: All were in the same area of the city, all needed work, all were considered bargains, we were always broke when we purchased them, and all came from God since He brought in every dollar. He usually made us wait until the last day, too. We joked that if our faith had not stretched, our life spans would have shortened.

We seemed always to have a waiting list, too. No sooner would we buy a house, fix it up, and hire counselors, than it would be overflowing and we'd have to begin again. We grew for many reasons: Our "students" told their friends about our cure rate, homey surroundings, and free legal aid; the courts referred troubled youths to us; parents told their children and relatives about us; parole officers recommended us; pastors sent counselees to us. I should never have worried about advertising!

By 1976 our horizons had moved beyond the Minneapolis area. Duluth, a two-hour drive north, was our first concern, since an unusual number of men, primarily alcohol and marijuana users, came to our Minneapolis center from up north. But that community was slow to respond at first. However, we were given the opportunity to buy an eighteen-room house in Milwaukee on McKinley Boulevard. On speaking engagements to Milwaukee, I'd learned from local policemen that at least eight thousand heroin addicts lived in their city.

Thus Milwaukee became our first Satellite responsibility. The city, eight hours' drive from Minneapolis, reflected the influence of Chicago's more sophisticated drug scene, and presented some of the most severe problems we faced: lesbianism, occultism, repeat offenders, heroin addiction, emotional disorders. In some ways the hard situations we faced in Milwaukee were training grounds for all our counselors, as those same problems eventually spread to infect every city in which we worked. (On January 1, 1981, the Milwaukee center became a Safe House for women—so named because it was a refuge for prostitutes going straight.)

Duluth was ready to move next. Appropriately, that Satellite took on an outdoor nature. Under the direction of John Halvorsen, a canoe enthusiast who had found Jesus while in the wilds of Canada and Alaska, men built homemade canoes, undertook outdoor camping and fishing expeditions, and in 1979 broke the existing record for canoeing the length of the Mississippi—over twenty-five hundred miles in forty-two days. (Regrettably, in 1980 the Duluth Satellite was forced to close its doors, due to insufficient local funding.)

An interval of two busy years passed before Willmar, a western neighbor about eighty miles away, began showing an interest. We felt, normally, that the wisest use of energy and funds meant locating our Satellites only in the larger cities, but God had placed in Willmar a man of prayer who wanted a center. Jack Bruggers was about sixty years old and knew nothing of drug addicts or the drug subculture, but he loved the Lord, he had a heart for young men in prison, and he believed in what God was doing at Midwest Challenge. He went to his neighbors and friends for support, prayed as only he can pray, and Midwest opened there in 1978. (Willmar has continued as an active, effective Center for men.)

In 1981, a Satellite opened in central Iowa; like Milwaukee, the pressing need there was for a Safe House for women. Queries came, too, from people in Florida, Texas, California, and other states.

Opening a Satellite meant more than finding a suitable residence and signing the papers, for a major element in our rehabilitation strategy was the work program. We had found that most junkies and delinquents did not know how to hold a job; teaching them healthy work habits would develop their sense of worth and accomplishment, we felt. Too, after graduation, many would be prepared to support themselves with a job skill.

147

So, in each center, students attended classes in the mornings and held down part-time jobs in the afternoons through our carefully structured work programs. The plan worked so well in Minneapolis that a business, Ark Products, was developed, marketing the students' woodcrafting work with handsome plaques and gift items.

In a way, Safe House had its roots in the same soil as did Midwest Challenge—it just grew a little more slowly. Even Kim, in the early days of the Project, had asked, "Is that house only gonna be for guys?" Obviously, young women were in need of the same help we offered young men. It was only natural, then, that our second Project home became the women's home. As we expanded, our women's work expanded, but there was no reason to add a separate title; we were all simply "Midwest Challenge." It remained that way for a long time.

But one day I flew to New York City and came back with a reason . . . a compelling reason. We had discovered the Minnesota Connection.

There is a section of midtown Manhattan called the Minnesota Strip, so named because of the many fair-haired hookers working there. Blond, fresh-looking, Scandinavian girls bring the highest prices on the New York market; some Minnesota pimps, upon discovering this fact, packed up their stables and went East. Many others moved into Minnesota to do their "shopping," then relocated in New York City in hopes of making it big. Often the "imported" pimp would use Minneapolis as a greenroom, a place to prepare both himself and his girls for the big money.

Prostitution is a highly competitive business and, as such, must offer a more and more attractive product to draw real money. That reason, coupled with man's corrupt nature which drives him to increasingly greater sin, created a horrifying trend toward the use of younger girls. When I met

Kim, that trend was slowly gathering impetus, but by 1977 it was epidemic. It was no trick, therefore, to stumble onto the Minnesota Connection, for the Missing Persons Bureau was jammed with names of girls who were disappearing from their homes and from the streets.

In light of the pimps' terrifying power over their girls, the only way we could persuade them to escape was to offer a place of protection and refuge—a Safe House.

The first three New York trips are recorded in my book, *The Minnesota Connection*. Very briefly, the first two trips were considered by some as failures, for not one girl returned to Minnesota with us. True, there were many mistakes made, perhaps the first of which was New York press involvement; we had hoped to slip unnoticed into New York as undercover agents. However, both trips received publicity; in fact, believing they were being blitzed by Minneapolis policemen, pimps sent their girls into hiding during our second visit. The third trip I arranged personally, taking only a van full of Midwest students, and we began seeing results. Given a chance to learn about us at last, young women gradually came to believe we could help them as we offered.

And so, Safe House was born. It was decided that Midwest Challenge, the drug program, would concentrate on the upper midwestern U.S., whereas Safe House, providing help and rehabilitation exclusively for women, would focus on the national front, though retaining its base of operations in Minneapolis.

"You're nuts, Palmquist," Pete greeted me one morning. "How much sleep did you get last night?"

"Five hours."

"And how much the night before that?"

"Five and a half."

"And before that?"

"Look, Pete, if I'd wanted to be attacked this morning, I'd

have had the Canine Division turned loose on me." I was in a horrible mood.

"Al," Pete went on earnestly, "you can't keep doing this. You're not big enough to go around anymore."

I scowled at him.

"Look at you!" Pete continued, throwing his arms up. He loved to exaggerate. "I'm your friend and I'm trying to talk to you, Palmquist. You're going to have to choose. Most people have enough trouble doing one job—you're trying to do two. Or three!"

"I don't need this, Pete," I complained.

"You need exactly this!" he countered. "You have what? three places out of town? And seven or eight houses here. You've been setting up all your Centers, all their work programs, hiring your staff and counselors, wading through all the paperwork, running all over the country with one meeting after another. Now you're making trips to New York and showing your mug on TV. Not to mention this 'Safe House' idea of yours! Where is it going to end, Al?"

I did not know where it would end. But I was not yet ready to give up either my career or my "kids." Both needed me. Or maybe I needed them.

»17«

The Ghost Is Back

I began smiling even before my eyes opened. No alarm had awakened me this morning, no meeting was scheduled for the evening, and I had the entire day off work. For the first time in months, I had slept in. And now the aroma of blueberry pancakes, as well as the friendly sounds of home, wafted luxuriously around my pillow.

Saturday! It was all mine.

After a huge breakfast I took down our bicycles, dusty from a winter's hibernation in the garage. Julie and Ricky, like frisky puppies, went off to find their friends, and Gayle was busy repotting some of her plants, so I set out alone. The sun was almost hot—a rarity for Minnesota on a May day—and the simple joy of biking through a grassy park became a tonic, coaxing away the stress and tension of past days.

We lived across the street from the shore of Lake Nokomis, one of Minneapolis' handsome lakes. In the distance, a tiny sailboat drifted on the brilliant blue water, and I watched it as I biked nearly all around Nokomis before stopping to rest. I had worked up a sweat, so I dropped, panting, onto the carpet of fresh soft grass to breathe the clean springtime air.

The scene was very still until I was startled to hear a tiny splash nearby. Then, one by one, from the protection of a mossy log, a family of graceful white ducks emerged. Momma Duck was intent on her bug-snatching lessons but the three frolicking youngsters were as struck with spring fever as I. When a game of tag broke out, I laughed in delight, sending them quickly for cover again.

I could not resist the temptation to lie back, fingers interlaced behind my head, and soak up the sun's penetrating warmth. Even thoughts of Midwest Challenge, constant companions for almost six years, left me in peace and I slipped into a lazy sleepiness as the water lapped at my feet.

Suddenly I bolted up, heart pounding furiously. Automatically reaching for the gun that was not there, I looked for whatever or whomever had frightened me. Though I could see nothing, a terrible sense of danger possessed me. The sun was gone, hidden behind a threatening cloud, and I was cold. Near panic, I grabbed my bike and peddled furiously away.

What was it? I asked myself, heart still racing. I had not seen anything unusual but something had scared me. I fought desperately for control but a salty wetness dropped to my cheeks and was whipped backward by the wind I created. I was sobbing with all the anguish of my soul now, and I knew . . . I knew what it was. It was a single thought, a single word, a single, searing pain that I had kept locked away. It had chosen an unguarded moment to burst forth in tears and agony, demanding recognition—demanding grief. The ghost was back.

Kimberly! I wept.

»18«

The Minnesota Strip and Beyond

She was the first person I saw when I walked into the Vice Office, and my heart stopped. "Kim!" I blurted as I hurried over. "What happened to you all this time? Where did you. . . ."

The girl finally looked up when she realized all the commotion was directed at her, and I hung there in midsentence, mouth gaping, examining her face. She looked like a Band-Aid commercial.

"Jennifer," she stated clearly, "not Kim." She laughed and extended her hand.

"I'm sorry," I fumbled. "You look like a girl I've been looking for."

"Story of my life," Jennifer said, seductively batting her lashes. Then she laughed again.

"Well, what happened to you?"

"Cut myself shaving?" she attempted.

I smiled, nodded, and surveyed the damage. Familiar little horseshoes tatooed her face, arms, shoulders, and upper chest above her halter top.

"A friend got mad at me," she said more quietly. "Broke my nose and eardrum and cut my head. Doc said I needed twenty-three stitches."

"A friend? Your friend knows a great way to use coat hangers, too, doesn't he?"

Jennifer looked up quickly.

153

"Where did you work?" I asked.

She paused for only a moment before naming a street in Manhattan.

"No kidding! Did you ever have pizza at Sergio's?"

Her face broke into smiles. "Sergio's? That's the best place in the country for pizza. How'd you know about that?"

"I worked in New York for a few years. I was a minister."

Jennifer raised her eyebrows in surprise. "A minister?" she echoed, taking in everything from my badge to my handcuffs to my .357 Magnum. "What are you now?"

"Both. I'm a cop but I still have a ministerial license. I like to preach."

She smiled. "So you were a minister, then you became a cop, but you're still a minister." She thought about this for a minute, then shook her head. "Mister, you're more mixed up than I am."

That broke me up. Some days I might agree with her.

"Do you know New York very well?" Jennifer asked.

"Well enough."

She leaned forward in her chair. "Ever heard of the Minnesota Strip?"

I nodded.

"It's hell," she said slowly, fixing her eyes on something from her memory.

I told her about the three trips.

"*You're* the one? You were on TV a couple 'a times, right? Oh, boy, I don't believe it! You caused a lot of trouble for us, you know that? Our pimps pulled us off the street when you 'Jesus pigs' were swarming all over the place. And then they'd give us a hard time 'cause we couldn't make any dough! Thanks to you!"

"What can I say? It's a living."

"Bet you didn't get many to bite, huh?"

"None the first two trips," I responded. "How'd you know?"

She shrugged. "Corruption. We figured you'd run into it, even with your own kind."

"Cops?"

"The same, honey. Payoffs are so common they're practically written into a cop's contract." She laughed bitterly.

"Did they bust you?"

"No, I finally got fed up. My old man sent me plane fare home after this beating." Jennifer inspected her injuries. "I'm going to press charges on that creep!"

"Well, when you were working the Strip I wonder if you happened to see a blond..."

She finished for me. "'... a blond girl named Kim.' There's a lot of blond on the Strip." She sighed. "I hate to even mention it, but there is this one girl... people said we could be twins." She looked up. "She won't be the right girl... you *know* she won't be the right one. Why torture yourself? Or maybe she's just on your Most Wanted list?" Jennifer chuckled.

If you only knew, Jennifer... if you only knew.

"Her name wasn't Kim, either. Lemme see...."

"Kitten!" I prompted. "Or something like that."

Jennifer looked up quickly, a smile breaking out, a light dawning.

"With a pimp named Jake, if he's still around. Ring any bells?"

Her mouth gaped open in delight. "I don't believe it! That just doesn't happen to people! I don't believe it! And she's from Minneapolis, too, I'm sure of it! Wow!"

I was nearly trembling. Seven years. *Seven years* we had waited for a break like this. "Where? Where was she? When did you see her last?"

"Just a few days ago. Working across from Sergio's, in fact! You just follow your nose, you'll find her."

I tried to find words to thank Jennifer but she waved me away.

155

"Save it. You don't even have her, yet."

She was right, we didn't. Some of the excitement drained away. But not all . . . not yet!

"Thanks again," I said.

"One thing . . ." Jennifer added as I turned to take care of the business that had brought me into the Vice Office, "you'd better not set your heart on having any of Sergio's pizza this trip. Jake's liable to stick a knife in your ribs."

Five days later I settled myself into the seat of a 747 headed east. This trip was nearly identical to the last, as a van load of students was to meet me on Eighth Avenue and Fifty-Second Street at seven o'clock that night. We had learned that the program kids could talk to hookers who wouldn't give cops the time of day.

There was, of course, one big difference in this trip. From my pocket I drew out the monogrammed handkerchief; older, yellowed a bit, but still the unfailing symbol it had always been. Sentimentally studying it, I thought of Gayle, who faithfully washed and ironed it with care. She was praying for Kim, I knew—and for me.

And then I sighed. There were a lot of "ifs." If Kimberly was still in New York. If this girl was really Kimberly Pringle. If Jennifer hadn't lied to me. If Jake didn't see me first and pull Kim off the street. If I didn't miss her. If she was still working the Strip. If she remembered me. If she *wanted* to go home. If she wasn't too stoned to care what she was doing. If she was still alive.

I leaned back and closed my eyes, determined to shut out the thoughts. I had had enough torment. From here on out, all I had left was hope.

I thought instead of Safe House, brooding yet spirited, sensitive yet hard—the infant sister in our Midwest Challenge family. She was a demanding child, unpredictable and often baffling.

My position as a police officer had worked in our favor

when Midwest Challenge began, establishing a visible image of authority and credibility. But the badge and blue uniform were not so well received by women from the streets. Too many of them associated cops with payoffs and corruption. "As long as you remain a cop," a hooker told me, "you won't find *us* at your front door!" If she was right, I would have no choice but to sacrifice my police work.

A decision was being forced from another direction, too. The Stenvig-Johnson team, as Charlie had warned, had been unseated, and the political winds he'd felt earlier had grown to gale force. I was in a tight spot.

Obviously, the ministries had grown too big for me to lead in my spare time, so some work time was spent with them, too. This created a question: Did Midwest Challenge and Safe House overstep the thin line between church and state?

A few from the political faction said we did.

I argued. Each time I went out to speak on behalf of Midwest, I was also an automatic public relations representative for the Minneapolis Police Department, I reasoned, so both fields of work benefited. It was absurd of the politicians to be rigid in their interpretation of the church/state issue. We were succeeding—juveniles were being rehabilitated—we were fulfilling our end of the deal. And we had real-life proof. I was, after all, only doing the job I had been assigned. And this brought up a philosophical dispute. How much influence could the police department afford to give politicians before it would begin affecting the quality of law enforcement? Could they insist that either a good police officer quit the force or a successful drug rehabilitation program be closed?

How ironic, that success could bully us in this way. If I had failed, I imagined, I'd have been left alone!

I picked up the newspaper to read the last of an eight-part series of articles about the Minneapolis Police Department. Here was another irritation. In the past few years the *Tri-*

bune had evidently turned on the police force. This series was a choice example. It had printed quote after quote from policemen, some of whom were my friends, who had never even been contacted by the paper, much less interviewed. This reporting was not merely biased, it was false.

During this time, too, the Youth Survey report came out—the misleading report which presented prostitution as a matter of choice. Other bits and pieces of unkind, slanted, innuendo-ridden reporting began accumulating, until there seemed no choice but to suspect a motive.

Turning to the Want Ads, I counted nearly a hundred ads featuring sexual services. They were disguised under terms like "massage parlors," "saunas," and "escort services." The *Tribune* was one of only a few major newspapers which would carry such ads. Considering the total dollar amount generated by the daily sale of that space, many of us were fairly sure we knew why the newspaper was at odds with the police force. It did not care to have its revenue tampered with.

Billy Graham had asked about Midwest Challenge one day. My services as bodyguard were often requested when he was in town, and he was quite interested in the work we were doing. When the Safe House ministry was described, Dr. Graham shook his head, "Be careful, Al. You're going deep into Satan's territory when you start tampering with prostitution. You'll uncover enemies you never dreamed existed." I was beginning to understand his concern.

A magnificent stream of sunlight caught my eye as it played with the white, clean clouds outside the jet's window. For a moment, I lost myself in the pure, still scene. I felt restored, remembering whose work we were doing, spiritually as well as literally rising above the battle. This was God's handiwork on display, and I could not help contrasting it with the corruption produced at the hand of man.

"Oh God," I prayed, "I don't know how I ever got mixed

up in this thing, but as long as You need me, I'll keep trying. I'd like to keep on being a cop, too, Lord, but I'm willing to give it up if that is the price You're asking to keep our homes open to the kids who need help."

Soon the jet began its descent. Back down to earth; back down to the battle lines. I had in my pocket a white handkerchief but not a white flag. The time was near to launch the attack.

We landed, and I taxied to midtown Manhattan, where I checked into the New York Hilton so that I could be within walking distance of the "front lines." I looked at my watch: ten minutes to five. Plenty of time before I had to meet the students at seven.

Dodging my way through the rush hour crowds, I felt giddy and lightheaded. "Maybe I need to eat . . . get my strength up," I thought. Everything around smelled wonderful: Polish sausages and pretzels from the little street vendors, great ethnic pizza from tiny shops, fragrant blooms from the flower carts, even the greenery and musky black earth from Central Park.

"Palmquist," I said to myself, wolfing down a crusty hunk of cheese-laden pizza. (In New York, pizza is often served nonstop in cafeteria style. You walk in, stand in line, buy a huge piece or two, then walk out.) "Palmquist, you've got to get hold of yourself! This is no time to lose your nerve!" But I *was* losing it: My stomach was in my throat, pizza and all, and my palms were sticky-wet.

Taking a deep breath, I crossed the street. A taxi, trying to skin through the intersection on a no-longer-yellow light, screeched to a halt only inches from me and a dozen others. The driver leaned out, shaking his fist and spouting angry Spanish at us. We disregarded him. This was New York, a singular city.

Four young women in eye-attracting clothes—bare backs or low cut fronts, bare midriffs or long-slit skirts—approached the men walking by with loud cries of, "Hey, honey, wanta have a real good time? How about a party, baby?" I was coming closer.

I could hear rock music, the volume growing louder at each step. I began to see pimps in dark glasses and big hats lingering watchfully in doorways or leaning on street lamps. I had reached the edge of the Minnesota Strip.

The scene unfolded before me as I walked more slowly. Sergio's was four or five blocks away but she could be anywhere. I was on the lookout for Jake, too. Though I'd never seen him, the Vice guys had provided a description, which included a facial scar—one of a cop's best clues in making an identification.

Briefly, I caught the eye of a black man who roughly fit Jake's description, although he had no scar. The man's dark eyes narrowed as he held my gaze, then he spit on the sidewalk. He knew I was not looking for entertainment. Whether he guessed my profession because of my walk or he sensed a certain "enemy" chemistry, I didn't know; but I found it unnerving. His appraisal seemed to me an aggressive act for a pimp, too. Obviously he considered me a trespasser on his turf.

From all appearances, the Strip did belong to owners of the sex industry. Each time I set foot there, I was startled again at the brazen mockery man had made of one of God's most beautiful gifts. I couldn't fathom how God could tolerate it. If He chose, He would wipe this street off the face of the earth! "But according to his mercy he saved us . . ." I recalled from Titus (3:5 KJV). This filth was nothing compared to the way we look in God's eyes. And still He loves us. I would never get over it.

A red and yellow sign appeared, blinking and enticing the pizza-hungry. Sergio's! My heart pumped furiously and I walked very slowly, afraid to look but afraid not to. Closer and closer I came, studying every face. My head screamed with the "ifs" now and my confidence vanished. Why had I come? I was a fool even to have tried this rescue stunt! Why had I told John and Millie? Get their hopes up, then dash them to the ground again!

A new torture came to my mind: What if I found her and then Jake tried to kill either or both of us? My blood ran cold. I fought off fear that was almost alive, threatening to strangle my very breath. Spiritual combat raged as I searched desperately, vainly.

She's not here! Wait . . . No! not that one, either. Maybe I was looking at her but not recognizing her! I was frantic.

When my inner screaming was at its loudest and my courage running out, I saw her.

Across from Sergio's, just as Jennifer had said. She stood back from the street, leaning against the wall, and if she hadn't looked up I'd have missed her again, for I'd already scanned that section of the street.

Gradually, I realized that the screaming in my head had stopped, I was not shaking anymore, and my heartbeat was slowing. I could breathe again. Peace was returning to my soul. We had nearly won this war, God and I. I couldn't even have explained how I knew her—her appearance had changed remarkably—but I was utterly certain that woman was Kimberly Pringle.

Exercising every shred of control, I stepped into a shadowed doorway where I could watch. She would eventually look at her pimp, I reasoned, and I needed to know his whereabouts before I could go further.

I was right—before long, I had established Jake's post. If he would only go check on one of his other girls before some john came and picked Kim up. Two, three, four minutes crept by. "Move, Jake!" I demanded silently. I was running out of time.

A trio of drunken men, pointing and laughing, seemed to be looking Kim's way and I realized it was time to do something. At least Jake did not know who I was . . . I hoped. I crossed the street, not letting Kim out of my sight. My hunch was right; the trio had begun walking toward her and several other girls nearby. I was at the opposite end of the block, so I had to pass Jake to get to Kim, a fact I found acutely uncomfortable. I walked quickly, keeping to the street side where I could mingle more easily. Just before I reached Jake he turned to face me and I caught my breath. But he only ambled slowly down the walk, his back to Kim. "Thank You, Lord," I breathed gratefully.

However, the trio of men had closed in on Kim. I tried walking faster but haste was impossible in the mass around me. I lost sight of her for a moment. When I could see again, Kim was walking away with one of the men. I had to catch her! I couldn't take any more chances of losing her.

Bumping some people in my hurry, I forced my way through the crowd until I was nearly behind Kim. Now what? Should I tap her shoulder and say, "Hi, Kim?" Should I create a disturbance with a loud cough or something? Should I pretend to ask directions to somewhere? Or should I just grab her and run?

As I agitated over the decision, Kim turned around to catch Jake's eye with a signal of some sort. She spotted me instantly and gasped. Continuing to walk, she stared for two or three long seconds, then turned her back on me and picked up her pace.

"No!" I groaned. She couldn't run away! Please, no! Helplessly I followed, watching in pain as Kim walked faster and faster. No, no, no! Not after all the waiting, not after all the years. We couldn't lose her again!

Kim led the john over to another hooker, who was applying very red lipstick with the aid of a mirrored compact. Kim whispered a few words to the hooker whose eyes first picked me out of the crowd, then fell on the drunken man. She nodded at Kim and began smiling and talking with the man as she took Kim's place.

Kim then turned to me. Her expression conveyed nothing, nothing at all. Quickly she searched for Jake, nodding slightly when she saw him watching us, I assumed, for I did not dare turn around. Then she slipped her hand through my arm and said quietly, "Act like a john."

We walked away. In total silence, neither of us trusting our voices, neither of us certain of safety, we quietly left the Minnesota Strip. The battle had been won. The waiting was over. We might celebrate later but that moment was reflective, pensive, somehow sad but filled with finality.

I mentioned the name of my hotel and Kim led the way, deciding which streets to walk, which alleys to take, which corners to turn. With a final darting look over her shoulder, she stepped into the wide, dark entrance of an abandoned building, drawing me after her. There she leaned back against the boarded up door and tried to take a deep breath. But her eyes filled with tears as she looked at me for several seconds, slowly shaking her head. Then great sobs churned and boiled to the surface to rack her body in convulsive spasms.

Kim wept for what could have been as I wept for what could yet be. I comforted her with joy and with tears: supporting, caring, sharing my strength with a precious, broken human being. No longer a child, this Kimberly Pringle . . . yet the child had returned from her seven-year exile to grieve in anguish and desolation. Strangely, perhaps, no words were necessary between us at first. I was struck with the utter simplicity of what had transpired, as though everyone had contributed his or her small part to a human drama which had been rehearsed a thousand times. I came, I found Kim, we walked away. Few could ever comprehend the profound weight of those words.

Kim accepted the white handkerchief eagerly, without

noticing its familiarity, and buried her face in it. When the intensity of her tears began to subside, she stood back, waiting for her composure to return. I watched in anticipation and she did not disappoint me. Shaking it open to find the driest spot, Kim spotted the monogram. Then she exclaimed in delighted surprise and dissolved in tears once more.

I laughed and patted her shoulder. "Come on, Kimberly Pringle, quit hogging the handkerchief. It's my turn."

Kim had tissues in her bag, too, enough for each of us to treat our sniffles and wet faces. I had prepared a special speech for the occasion, so I cleared my throat heartily. Kim waited expectantly. "Kim," I began, "would you like some french fries?"

She smiled nostalgically and gave me a bear hug. "Do french fries solve everyone's problems, Copper?" she asked.

"Nope. Only yours."

She powdered her nose and adjusted her face a bit more, then moved out of the shadows and into the doorway where she carefully surveyed the street. Satisfied that we had not yet been discovered, she looked toward the sky and sighed deeply. It was an old, weary, worn sigh that had waited a long time to find expression. Then we hurried to the Hilton.

The dining room was crowded, so Kim slipped into the ladies room while I waited for a table. Finally we were seated. I checked my watch and noted with shock that the entire, exhausting transaction had taken only sixty-five minutes. The longest sixty-five minutes of my life, undoubtedly. Suddenly I was famished and my knees were wobbly.

"I want you to know something," I said, leaning toward Kim. "I've aged ten years today."

Kim smiled a little but her bottom lip began to quiver and I was immediately sorry I'd said it. So I changed the subject. I gave her a brief history of Midwest Challenge and Safe House, telling her why I was in town. "I have to meet the students in less than an hour," I said.

Kim had asked questions about the ministry, but at that remark she sat quietly, eyes on her hands in her lap. "Doesn't give us much time to talk," she commented. She had given me an opening.

"I would like to put you on a plane tonight and send you back home, to John and Millie's. When you're ready, you can go into Safe House if you like, Kim."

She fidgeted with her napkin. "I don't know, Al. It's been a long time and I've done a lot of things. Do you think they will still like me?"

I took out a pen and worked a multiplication problem on a paper coaster. Kim watched, fascinated. "I'd forgotten how goofy you were," she laughed. "What are you doing?"

"Kim," I answered, "the way I figure it, John and Millie have prayed for you at least two thousand five hundred and fifty times since you left. That's only once a day, so it would be more, actually. They have called me about two hundred times to ask if I'd heard anything. They keep a picture of you next to your Bible on the piano —it's practically a shrine! Your clothes are still hanging in the back of your closet. And they have listened to your first prayer who-knows-how-many times!" (I had to explain the tape recording to Kim.) "So the answer is, 'No, I don't think they still like you; I know for sure they still love you!' Same goes for me, by the way, in case you wondered."

Her face softened briefly, almost in disbelief.

"Were you out looking for girls to take back to Safe House when you found me?" Kim asked finally. "I still can't get over how. . . ." But her voice dropped off and she did not finish.

I explained how I "happened" to run across Jennifer the day I "happened" to be in the Vice Office, how I "happened" to be coming back to New York anyway, how I "happened" to pick Kim out in a huge crowd after seven years, and how I "happened" to assume she wanted to be rescued. "Yes, Kim," I said, "I just 'happened' to be in the neighborhood and thought I'd find you and send you home, ho-hum. Nothing to it, really."

A tear sparkled on her cheek.

"I have a lot of questions," I said. "Feel like talking about it?"

She closed her eyes for a moment, then nodded and sighed deeply. With her napkin she whisked away a tear, then said, "I need to talk about it, Al. I've made a mess of things and I'm so afraid you and John and Millie will hate me. But I have to know . . . I just have to know."

"Kim, we would never hate you, no matter what. . . ."

She looked up quickly, a rebuke on her face. "Don't say that yet. Let me tell you first—please, Al! I want you to understand before you make rash promises." With that, Kim looked over the dining room crowd to be sure we were not being watched, and then began her story in a subdued voice.

"While Billy was in jail, he and Jake cut a deal for me. Billy wanted me dead or out of town before his trial, and Jake wanted me to work for him. So Jake started asking questions and found out I was at the Jesus People house. He watched it for a couple of days and saw me go out to buy some suntan lotion—did Millie tell you?"

I nodded.

"Jake had a buddy with him and they cornered me in an alley on my way home. Naturally I tried to run but with both of them. . . ." Kim shook her head as she relived the struggle. "So the other guy shoved me into the back seat and Jake handed him a syringe. I really screamed when I saw it because I thought for sure I was dead when they stuck that thing into me. I remember Jake giving me an awful beating but it gets fuzzy. . . ."

I interrupted. "Jake's stuff was gone by the time I got to the apartment—he must have split right away. You were both seen down on Fifth sometime that night."

166

"Maybe Jake dropped his buddy off," Kim said. "I never saw him after that."

"What about Jake's other girls?" I asked.

Kim shrugged. "Part of the deal. Jake only had two at that time, so Billy traded me and a pile of drugs for Jake's girls. But Jake told me Billy got sent up after all—that true?"

"Yes."

"So he lost out on the deal." After a thoughtful moment, Kim added, "We all lost out on the deal."

Then she continued. "Jake must have used a lot of those drugs on me because I don't remember much about driving to New York. Every time I started to come around, he would pull off the toll road and give me a shot or make me swallow something. I guess he didn't want any trouble from me.

"I was still foggy when we got to this guy's place here in the city. Jake dragged me to the door, telling me to be real good to his friend because we were broke and needed a place to stay. Good to him! I couldn't even stand up by myself! And he was some kind of creep!" Kim shuddered. "He had a stable of about twenty girls and it smelled like a stable in there, I'll tell you! There was trash and garbage all over the place, and cockroaches everywhere! We even had rats in the apartment awhile.

"Well, anyhow, so I was leaning on the wall with all Jake's clothes and boxes around me, when Bennie came over to 'check out the new merchandise.' He told two of his girls to strip me and when I began crying and fighting them off, he pulled out his switchblade. I thought, *If he'd kill me with that thing, I'd run!* but I figured he would cut on me, instead, 'til I cooperated, so I stood still. I was so scared that I got kind of numb all over. Bennie examined every inch of me—said he didn't want any diseased stock, like I was a cow or something—and then he raped me right in front of Jake and the girls. I learned that day how to turn off all my

167

feelings when I wanted to, a trick I used every time I went to work. After awhile, it became automatic. Except for the beatings. They hurt too much; I couldn't stop the real bad pain.

"Jake was mad but didn't even try to get Bennie to quit. When Bennie realized how Jake felt, he laughed and laughed—it was a hideous laugh—and decided I needed to be initiated into the 'big time in the Big Apple.' I'm not going to tell you the twisted, sick, bizarre stuff Bennie did or had done to me but it went on for two hours. Part of the time I was even throwing up but still he kept on. And he kept laughing! I thought of about a thousand ways to kill him that afternoon.

"Finally he told some of the girls to clean me up and get me ready for work. Do you believe it? I had to go to work that same night! I must have blacked out, but one of the girls was holding a needle when I opened my eyes again, and I started feeling really high. She stayed with me on the street that night and gave me uppers when I needed them, too. Every time I had a customer I was afraid I would be sick. And all the time I kept telling God I was sorry for whatever I had done and wouldn't He please get me out of there?

"By four in the morning I couldn't even walk. The older hooker who was taking care of me helped me get back to the apartment, where she handed me a dirty blanket and a pillow. 'Not enough beds,' she said. 'Bunk anywhere.' Someone was already on the sofa but by that time I didn't care where I slept, so I just collapsed in a corner. I was too tired to open my eyes when Jake came in behind us, so he came over and yanked my pillow away, demanding his money and telling me not ever to go to sleep without first giving him his money. I motioned toward my purse, which made Jake so mad he kicked me in the stomach. 'Jake don't go trackin' down his own cash, baby!' he said. 'You get up an' get me my dough, right now!'

"I couldn't breathe for a few seconds but I crawled over, opened the purse, and got out all the money for Jake. In the meantime, Jake put his foot on my pillow and tossed my blanket over his arm. He made me wait until he had counted the bills. I was shivering and felt so sick—all I wanted to do was die. Finally Jake exploded. 'Five hundred bucks? Is that all? You gotta do better than that! You go back out there and. . . .'

"I pleaded and I cried. I told him I couldn't work any more that night and I would do better tomorrow. I just didn't know the ropes yet and it was my first night. . . if he would just give me a chance! I was hysterical. He looked at me then and started to smile. He reminded me of a snake when he grinned that way. Anyway, he said he would go easy on me just this once if I would say thank you real nice and sweet. I would have done anything.

"Well, you can guess the rest. He kept making me call him my 'Big Daddy,' my 'main man,' and I had to promise that I loved him and would be good to him always. He held my face and stared into my eyes while he sort of chanted things he wanted me to repeat again and again and again. It was like he got into my brain and took over, Al. I thought what he wanted me to think, acted the way he wanted me to act, went where he wanted me to go, and said what he wanted me to say.

"Jake used a combination of pain, very little sleep, drugs, and this little hypnotic game to turn me into an unthinking, uncaring, unquestioning slave. It didn't all happen that first night, of course, and for a long time I fought him in my head. But I was thirteen, Al—thirteen! And I finally just gave in. You can only take so much until you begin to crack."

I nodded my head. I did not understand how it happened, but I believed it could and did, not only to Kimberly but to many others who had tried to explain it, as well. "Go on," I urged.

"I went through a lot of stages over the years," Kim said, trying to condense a million moments into one conversation. "For a little while I thought about escaping but I was afraid. I didn't care about getting killed, but if you knew all the ways pimps have of torturing you! That worried me most.

"And then I stopped thinking. I was just too tired to care what happened to me as long as I made enough money to avoid the beatings. If God doesn't care enough to get me out of this hell, I thought, why should I? So I quit praying, too. I didn't have the nerve to get mad at God so I didn't think about Him. That stage lasted a long time. Jake and Bennie started running ads in a smut newspaper—three ads, each at a different phone number and each featuring a different kind of sex—and we had to work twenty-four hours a day. We learned to grab a few hours' sleep whenever and wherever we could. We took lots of drugs, then; drugs to help us work faster and harder, and drugs to help us get to sleep in a hurry. I was a zombie.

"Sometime in '74 one of the regular let's-clean-up-New York campaigns zeroed in on the Strip, so Jake decided to pull up stakes. He took me and two other girls all the way to Los Angeles. Something happened on that trip that started my next stage. Jake had business in Minneapolis, so we stopped for a couple of hours."

"You were in town and didn't call?" I asked.

Kim held up her hand. "Hold on, Al. I called my dad. He was at work and they weren't going to let me talk to him but I told them I was his daughter, I hadn't seen him for several years, and I just wanted to see how he was doing. In the back of my mind, I had worked out a way to give Jake the slip if Dad asked me to come back. Anyway, Dad finally came on the line. 'Dewey Pringle,' he said, all stern and businesslike—I mean, they *must* have told him who was calling, you know?—and I said, 'Hi, Dad, it's Kimberly.' 'Kimberly who?' he asked. I laughed, like it was a joke. 'Quit kiddin' around.

Kimberly your daughter, that's Kimberly who!' I said. 'Listen here,' he said, 'I got no daughter named Kimberly. I heard there was a slut prostitute by that name but she's no daughter of mine. If you ever meet her, you tell her not to call me until she's ready to apologize and clean up her act.' He waited for me to answer, but all the bitterness and resentment came flooding back and I couldn't say a word. He owes me an apology, too, I thought, and his act has never been cleaned up!

"So, I slammed the door of my heart shut on him," Kim sighed. "I still blame him for so much, Al."

"What about the rest of your family, Kim? Did you ever try to look up your mother? Or call your two sisters?"

"Didn't John tell you? I talked to my mother one day while I was still at the Jesus People house—Millie thought it would be a good idea to let her know where I was and tell her about my decision to trust the Lord. But Mom called me a religious fanatic and said she didn't have time for me in her new life. I even asked if I could come and visit her and she said, 'No, that wouldn't be a good idea.' Joey (that's her new husband) didn't like the thought of having extra people around the house. I didn't like to be thought of as 'extra people,' so I shut that door, too.

"And my sisters? That first week in New York I asked a john if he would go get me something to drink and then I put a long distance call on his bill while he was out of the room. I asked my sister to wire me some money to get home. I begged her. But she said, 'Oh, I could get the money, I'm sure. But you got your sassy little self into that mess, you just get yourself out! Nobody was there to help me when I needed it, baby sister!' she said. And she wouldn't even ask my other sister for me. Not that it would have done any good; they're too much alike.

"You and John and Millie are the only people I know that I could have gone to for help..."

171

I started to interrupt but Kim shushed me.

". . . and I knew you would have done everything possible. But Al, I was trash. I *was* a prostitute! I was hooking for a living! I was doing the very thing you were trying to stop and I was too ashamed to face you. I had let John and Millie down, too, and I believed it was up to me to get straightened out before I came crawling back to you.

"The worst part is, after my entire family had thrown me out of their lives, I turned my back on everyone but Jake. My mind got all distorted. You and John and Millie were living in a lily-white, never-never world that I didn't belong to. I had started life as an unwanted child, my sisters became hookers, then I became a hooker, then my own family rejected me—what right did I have to think that three total strangers could come along and show me a higher, holy way to live? You three had somehow made a mistake—you had picked the wrong girl to love. I looked back on those two months as a dream, a fluke, a life I wasn't worthy of. I would have to grub it out until I had made my own way in this world. I couldn't count on help from anyone, not family, not strangers, not God.

"Not even Jake. But he was my ticket to independence, so I went to work like never before. I did anything to make dough. I helped kidnap young girls and train them. I was a good teacher, too." Kim's voice had taken on a hardness; her very words caused me to wince in pain.

"Our relationship changed at that point. At last, I was using Jake. He became more like my manager than my pimp and didn't dare beat me anymore. I made piles of money, which meant power. If he didn't arrange enough contacts, or if his deals didn't pay enough, or if he stole any of my money, I took away one of his 'toys.' One time I burned his favorite three-piece suit. Boy, was he mad! But we had a two-way deal going and he knew he had to hold up his end of it.

"During that time, we moved all over the country. I

worked Vegas, Hawaii, Miami—anywhere we heard there was money. And I did any kind of work, too. We spent the cash almost as soon as I earned it, so we were always on the prowl for bigger bucks, but we had enough money to stay high all the time. We began making mistakes, however. Jake usually looked after the girls we had working the streets, but he was so strung out one night that they took off with the Mercedes and all our cash. He tried to find them but couldn't. I got a little scared of my drug habit at that point but I couldn't stop.

"We ended up in New York nine months ago, almost as broke as the day we left. Jake went into treatment to kick his habit, but I was too afraid. I thought that I couldn't exist without my pills and needles.

"I used an old street trick one night: Steal a customer's hotel key, especially those from the fancy hotels, wait a couple of weeks, then go back and lift any valuables that can be traded or fenced for drugs. I must have looked pretty bad with all the junk I'd been putting into my body, because an undercover cop tailed me to the room the night I decided to go back for the payoff, waited until my pockets and purse were full of jewelry and cash, then busted me.

"I was locked up for four months. At the time I thought it was the end of my life but, looking back, I can see how God planned every move. For the first few days I was kept in an old city jail where I kicked my habit." Kim braced her elbows on the table, then buried her face in her open hands and took several long, deep breaths. When she looked up her face reflected the strain of the experience. "I was almost a goner, Al," she said. "It was like getting a two-day beating from the inside out. I didn't believe I'd ever make it. The cops just let me scream. It didn't matter to them whether I left to go to prison or the morgue. I suppose they see a lot of withdrawal, but still . . .

"Then I was shipped off to a state jail which was no fine

hotel, either. My first day there I was sitting in the rec room when this big, forty-three-year-old hooker came over, grabbed a fistful of my hair and said, 'O.K., little Kitty-Cat, you'll do just fine.' I yanked my hair from her hand and said something nasty, so she dragged me out of the chair and started pounding on me. Oh, was I hot! I said to myself, 'This is it! I'm gonna kill myself, because I won't be used by any more pimps or johns or sick whores!'

"She hauled me off to her cell and dumped me on the cot where I curled up into a hard ball. The minute she touched me, I planned to bite and scratch and kick—whatever it took to keep her away. I felt her sit down beside me, then she whispered, 'Knock it off. I've just done you a big favor, kid. I'm not what you think, but you can save yourself a lot of grief if you play along.' When I looked at her, thinking she was some weird flipp-o, she smiled and shrugged her shoulders. 'I'm not a lesbian, honey. But I like to keep that a secret so nobody will hassle me or my girls.' 'Your girls?' I asked. 'Yeah. You see, I can usually spot a kid who wants to break out of prostitution. Am I wrong?' I looked at her for a long time because I couldn't believe what she had said. Finally I answered, 'No, lady, you're not wrong. I hope you're straight because that's the best line I've heard all day!'

"The next few weeks she listened to my story and protected me from a lot of the rot that goes on in prisons, then gradually began to tell me about what Jake had done to my head as well as what I had done to myself. She was incredible! She knew exactly how to describe the hatred I had toward myself, the fear I had of pimps, and the disgust I had for my family. She even explained why I felt I couldn't call you for help. And little by little, she showed me how to regain my humanity. She made me believe in life again.

"She didn't know anything about the Lord, but I believe with all my heart the Lord sent the best person He could find, under the circumstances, to get me started back toward

Him. I was afraid to start praying because I felt like such a hypocrite; besides, I still couldn't figure out why God didn't answer my prayers when I was first kidnapped. But I knew this much: I had tried living life my way and I wasn't about to try it again!

"One night, lying on my cot, I told the Lord everything in my heart. I apologized for all the sins I'd committed against Him and asked His forgiveness, then I told Him He could have whatever was left of my life. I told Him that I didn't understand why He seemed to let me down that once but I had let Him down so many thousands of times that I'd be willing to wait until I got to heaven to hear the answer! 'Anyhow,' I told Him, 'You're all I have left, and even if You don't answer me, You are stuck with me because no matter what happens, I will find a way out of prostitution and start living for You again!' "

Kim stopped, her face flushed, and took a drink of water. "That woman in prison gave me the name of a friend who would take me in until I could get back on my feet. But Jake met me at the gate the day I was released. I figured this was my first test from God, to see if I meant business or not. Jake was meaner than ever since he kicked his habit, and he already had a new stable of three other girls. Clearly, he felt he was back in control. He said he had some old scores to settle with me.

"Jake beat me real bad that first night and I felt some of the old fears returning, so I pleaded with the Lord to help me get out before I began to go back on my promise. I was so desperate. Jake had taken to carrying a gun, and he watched me every second—I was as much a prisoner with him as I had been in jail. But God sent three signs to hang onto. Jake never beat me again, Al. I guess he thought his gun was intimidating enough. And he let me read my Bible. I had managed to scrounge one up in prison. You'd have to know Jake to understand what a big deal that was. Jake had a thing about 'religious' people—you should have heard what he said about you! But he never made me give up my Bible."

"How long have you been back on the Strip?" I asked.

Kim counted. "Nine days now. Jennifer's last day on the Strip must have been my first day back."

I paid the check, then, since Kim and I had to move fast if we expected to meet the students by seven. Some folks might criticize Kim for going back to the streets, I thought. But those folks had probably never had a gun at their backs, either. Besides, Kim was still a baby in her faith—two months plus nine days of actual growth.

"Say, Kim," I said when we were hurrying toward our destination, "you told me God sent you three signs but you only mentioned two. What was the third?"

Kim stopped dead in her tracks and turned to face me with a smile. Yet another tear found its way down the side of her cheek. "I'm looking at it, Al Palmquist!" she said triumphantly. "I'm looking at it!"

»19«

Of Faith and Friendship

"**M**illie?" I shouted. Kim and I were at LaGuardia Field waiting for the last flight to Minneapolis. "Millie, is that you?"

"Yes, this is Millie," I heard faintly.

"Millie, it's Al and I'm calling from New York. I wonder if you have a nice clean bed for an old friend?" It was still hard to keep back the tears.

"Aaeeoouuyyii!" I heard, not so faintly. But I'd known Millie too long to let the unearthly sound surprise me. She probably had her apron in shreds by now, too.

John came on the line. "Al, is that you? Millie's in a state here! Whatever did you tell her?"

"I just wanted to know if you two have a nice clean bed for an old friend, that's all."

"Oh, Al, you don't mean it! Well, of course you mean it! Praise the Lord! Is Kim there? Is she O.K.? Can we just hear her voice again?"

I motioned for Kim to take the phone. "Hurry," I whispered.

"Hi, John," she said timidly. There followed a series of one-word answers: "Uh-huh, yes, O.K., sure, uh-huh, yeah, no, no, yes..." before she turned the phone back over to me.

I gave John the flight information and hung up. "Let's go, Kim, or you'll miss your plane," I said. At the gate I

reminded her that I would be home in two days, but that
John and Millie would be at the airport to meet her and
would take care of everything she might need. "Are you
nervous?" I asked.

Kim nodded. "John sounded so loving and forgiving. I'm
having a hard time believing all of this is real. I'm not going
to wake up and find out it's a wonderful dream, am I?"

I laughed and hugged her shoulders. "With me in it? More
than likely it would be a nightmare!"

So Kim went home. The students and I talked to hundreds
of hookers in the next forty-eight hours and distributed our
"Hotline to Freedom" cards—cards bearing our phone number and a promise of transportation to a place of safety. A
number of girls listened to the gospel presentation and
several responded. We were saddened that none felt free to
return to Minnesota with us, but they accepted our Hotline
cards and a great deal of telephone counseling was done in
the days that followed.

"John, how is Kim doing?" I asked one day about a week
after her homecoming. John had dropped by our house with
a small white envelope in his hand.

"You'd better come see for yourself," he replied, handing
the envelope to Gayle. "Millie's trying to plan a surprise
party for Kim but the whole house is in a dither. I had to get
out of there for a breather!"

"It's Kim's birthday?" Gayle asked.

"Not for five months, but Millie will celebrate anything,
anytime!" John chuckled. "Anyway, we can celebrate all the
birthdays we missed."

"What a nice idea!" Gayle exclaimed. "Well, Al doesn't
have to work Saturday afternoon so you can count on us.
Shall I call Millie?"

"No, no, we're already counting on you two—I asked Al for
his schedule and Millie planned the party around him."

Gayle laughed. "I know exactly what you mean, John," she
said.

"Now don't forget to bring Kim a big present," John directed. "None of this five-dollar stuff." And then he was off.

Saturday afternoon found us at John and Millie's front door just before 2:30. "How am I going to hide this box so Kim doesn't see it?" Gayle wondered.

Just then the door opened and Kim's smiling face greeted us. "Why, Mr. and Mrs. Palmquist, how lovely to see you," she said graciously. "Welcome to my surprise party! Do come in . . . and may I relieve you of that heavy-looking gift you're hiding, Gayle?"

The party went along in the same festive, lighthearted manner until time for the cake to be presented. Millie spent an unusual amount of time in the kitchen just then, refusing to allow anyone to help. Finally John called for everyone's attention, and Millie appeared at the dining room entrance with a spectacular offering. The cake was the largest I had ever seen, with fourteen pink candles, fifteen yellow ones, sixteen blue ones, seventeen green ones, eighteen white ones, nineteen silver ones and twenty gold ones, each flickering with life. The message, enhanced by roses and graceful vines, read, "To Kim, Loved and Never Forgotten." A series of "Happy Birthdays" and "Welcome Homes" framed the creation.

Everyone "ooh-ed" and "aah-ed," then the familiar "Happy Birthday" was sung to Kim, who stood by, eyes glistening with tears in the light of the dancing flames. The cake, at least, had been a complete surprise.

The only speech she could utter was, "I thank you all for love, even when I didn't know what to do with it. Today I know what to do with it: Return it. And so, I love you . . . each of you."

In contrast to Kim's exuberant spiritual growth under John and Millie's care once again, Safe House trudged. The project grew, but not quickly. I continued my attempt to ride out the controversy over the separation of church and state, and I continued my attempt to be both policeman and executive director. The conflicts were slowly wearing me out.

Gayle and I decided to spend the Christmas of 1979 in Florida with our family. "Your bones are getting too old for our Minnesota winters, huh?" friends teased. And the sun baking our bodies did feel exhilarating when I considered that a two-hour jet trip north would drop us into the midst of an icy blizzard. But the relief came from more than that. I needed to get away, to think, to make the final decision.

Month after month I had cornered the girls who had come to Safe House. "Do you think my badge and uniform hurt the Safe House image?" I asked new students. Almost all agreed that they did. They explained that girls on the street are acquainted only with Vice cops, and the cops who compromised their standards were usually Vice cops. Vice cops, they said, were constantly exposed to temptations: available women, available booze, and available money and goods. Classic temptations.

Even in the face of all the corruption receiving the sensational publicity, I still believed policemen were, over all, the most honest of all men. The girls did not believe that, but I did. Besides, I loved police work. I also liked the idea that I was well over halfway toward a lifetime police pension. Maybe I was afraid to quit. Joseph Wambaugh, writer, author of TV's "Police Story," and former Los Angeles police sergeant, said once on nationwide television that he dreamed about police work every night after he quit. Maybe being a cop was like being Irish—you can never really stop being one.

The struggle, simply put, was that on one hand I wanted to talk God into letting me remain a policeman; on the other hand, I sincerely wanted God's mind on the subject. And I was coming to see the real conflict.

One morning I went for an early jog on the beach. Thoughts of the decision, as usual, dominated my mind even as I ran. After two miles, I stopped, puffing hard, and looked into the sky. "God," I shouted impatiently, "what should I do?" Like a spoiled child, I was demanding an answer, but I was so tired of wondering. So tired!

My eyes looked over the beauty around me, from the beach to the gently lapping waves, to the sandpipers to the hazy fog rolling off toward the bay; and I heard a word: *Quit*. It came again: *Quit*. And again: *Quit*.

Who am I to say God cannot speak? Even a skeptical cop can hear from God if God chooses to speak . . . from his Spirit to ours, at least.

I walked back to our hotel and told Gayle the decision had been made. In her usual supportive style, Gayle responded. "Good. I think quitting is a good idea. I am with you, honey, and I certainly want you to obey God. Now, can we go have breakfast?"

Never once since have I doubted that word from God. We flew home to the land of ice and snow and I turned in my resignation. The action hurt, yes, but I had complete peace about it and, Joseph Wambaugh notwithstanding, I did not compulsively dream about police work every night.

A few days later I pulled up in front of Safe House and greeted a youngster named Katy. "Hey, Al," Katy yelled, "we have three new girls in the program. What'd you do, quit the police force?"

"Yeah," I yelled back, "that's exactly what I did!"

Katy's mouth dropped open. Naturally, the girls had not been enrolled within the half hour of my resignation and final paper-signing. But Katy became excited anyway. "Oh, Al, that's God telling you you've done the right thing. That's His way of reassuring you!"

My resignation made the front page of the Minneapolis *Tribune*. "Good," I thought. "Maybe the street kids will see this and know that I am so serious about the ministries that I intend serving them fulltime." And while there have been moments of nostalgia, perhaps wistfulness, the rewards of reaching desperate young men and women with help and with Jesus Christ far outstrip any long-lasting attachments I had made to police work.

I watched for a new trend at Safe House and was not disappointed. For whatever reason, whether due to my resignation, having available more quality time to spend in ministry, or some other reason entirely, our programs have continually had a waiting list since 1980. A list of young people waiting for the chance to give God a chance at their busted up, scarred up lives.

"Al," my secretary whispered as I hurried toward my combination Midwest Challenge and Safe House office one day, late for an appointment. "There's a really beautiful woman in your office. And she didn't leave her name. . . ."

"It's O.K.," I whispered back. "I'm expecting her." Then I winked and opened my door.

"Kim, how are you? Sorry I'm late," I said, "but I'm almost as busy now as when I was a cop, too! Say, you look terrific!"

"I am terrific, Al. Really terrific." Her radiant smile convinced me.

Kim had spent two weeks with John and Millie, resting and getting her feet back on the ground, before she enrolled as a Safe House student. There, like all students, she had concentrated on structured Bible study which gave her the basics of the Christian's walk with the Lord. Building her spiritual muscles little by little, bit by bit, she put her past behind her forever. An eager student, she not only made a project of studying the Word of God, but earned her General Equivalency Diploma (G.E.D.) in lieu of the usual high school diploma.

Not all students were ready to handle their own lives again after the initial three-month program, but Kim was. I'd helped her locate a small apartment and she had landed a

182

promising job. Hired by a national airline, she was trained in their stewardess school to become a skillful, efficient hostess, looking after the needs and comforts of others.

"Hey," Kim said, snapping her fingers in my face to bring me back from my musings. "You're not listening to me."

"Oh, I'm sorry, Kim. I was just thinking of a mixed-up kid I used to know. Wonder whatever happened to her?"

"She grew up. And she joined a great church in south Minneapolis where she found someone she wants you to meet soon."

"Is that what this is all about?" I asked. *"Someone?"*

In answer, Kim held up a manicured hand on which she proudly displayed a sparkling, elegant diamond ring. Her eyes had a matching sparkle of their own.

"Kim, it's beautiful. Congratulations!" I said from the bottom of my heart.

"Oh, Al, I can't believe it! Mike is so wonderful, so good to me, and I'm in love, Al! Imagine me, in love! Oh, isn't it exciting? It's a high I don't ever come off!"

"Say, I have just the cure for that, Kim," I said enthusiastically, jumping up and grabbing my wallet.

"Oh, no . . . ," Kim groaned, "not. . . ."

"French fries!"

Afterword

The book you have just read was written to expose and define a national disaster of which few people are aware. It tells the truth about prostitution in America, especially regarding the treacherous recruitment of children and teens.

Most Americans have probably seen a pimp without knowing so. And most average teenagers have probably been observed by a pimp in one circumstance or another. When Kimberly's story took place, pimps typically recruited young women in the alluring, dazzling downtown areas of larger cities, places usually preferred by lone, unsuspecting runaways.

But by the time Kimberly's story was written, the scene began to change. Pimps put away the flashy, stereotypical outfits and took to wearing handsome sweater-and-slacks combinations or popular sports clothes. Their recruiting grounds moved into the suburbs, especially into large shopping malls, where thousands of kids hang out unchaperoned with their friends. Pimps found that suburban areas and shopping centers are seldom heavily patrolled by the police; even the security guards have little or no police training and carry no firearms.

The "Pipeline" changed, too. Added to the New York market were Miami, Dallas, Houston, Los Angeles, Denver,

Tampa, and the most recent hot spot as of this writing, Las Vegas.

As man's corrupt nature runs more and more out of control, he demands increasingly younger victims for his insatiable appetites. Recent attention to homosexuality has given rise to male prostitution as has never before been witnessed in America's history. Tonight, eight- and nine-year-old boys and girls will work the streets of most major cities in our country.

Midwest Challenge and Safe House remain dedicated to rescuing desperate youngsters from the streets and offering them a new, clean life through the power of Jesus Christ. We rely solely on the support of individuals who share our anguish and are willing to help us help them.

If you have been moved by Kimberly's story—and I trust that you have—you may want to receive our newsletters, which bring regular updates on the drug and prostitution scene and advise further ways to stop the horrible evils which are sweeping our country. Write to us at the address on page 188.

Maybe you are one of the trapped kids to which we have referred. Prostitute, addict, homosexual, alcoholic, or drug abuser, we would like to help you. Please get in touch with us.

Despite the terrifying picture we have painted through the story of Kimberly Pringle, take heart: There are ways to prevent youth prostitution.

PARENTS:

1. *Set a proper example.* Take your children to church, don't just send them. Live the kind of life you expect them to duplicate. The magazines you read, the television shows you watch, the way you treat each other are what your children are taking in.

2. *Teach children the Word of God.* Give them a sound foundation upon which to build their lives.

3. *Love your kids and make them feel loved.* Accept them emotionally (laugh and joke with them) as well as physically (hug them, give them a real pat on the back sometimes).

4. *Keep your promises.*

5. *Listen to what they're saying.* Listen to what they're not saying, too.

6. *Know what your kids are doing, feeling, thinking.* It takes time and an uncritical attitude, but they will open up in a nonthreatening environment.

7. *Provide healthy activities to keep them occupied.* And join in—often.

KIDS:

1. *Don't go places alone.* Take a friend or stay with your group.

2. *Avoid using public restrooms.* Instead, use the ladies' or men's rooms in restaurants, theaters, etc.

3. *Don't allow strangers to engage you in conversation.*

4. *Avoid eye contact with strangers* whom you suspect are watching you. You can meet plenty of new friends at school, church, youth group, Bible studies, and through other friends.

5. *Be alert to pimp activity* in shopping centers, downtown areas, bus depots, bars, discos, even school sports activities—anywhere you are likely to be alone for periods of time.

6. *Don't run away from home! Don't run away from home! Don't run away from home!* Even if you're honestly being treated unfairly, there are more effective and far less dangerous ways to deal with your parents. Talk to your pastor, a school counselor, a favorite teacher, or older

friend. Or contact us and we can recommend a helping ministry near you.
7. *Let the Lord control your life*. His Word will steer you away from trouble. At the very least, don't surrender to the influence of alcohol, drugs, or a too-powerful peer group.

The Love Factor is a fictionalized account, but only because the truth had to be rearranged to protect individuals who have been hurt far too much already. Tonight, in the cities and towns of America, Kimberly's story will come true thousands and thousands of times. Most of those stories, however, will have no happy endings. No one has yet told these kids about the Love Factor.

> Al Palmquist, Executive Director
> MIDWEST CHALLENGE, INC./SAFE HOUSE
> 8200 Grand Avenue South
> Bloomington, MN 55420